Down the
BRISTOL AVON

AUDREY

D0130345

Cover: Bath: New Bridge, 1830

Limpley Stoke Valley from Dundas Aqueduct

Whaddon Bridge, near Melksham

Down the
BRISTOL AVON

Including 14 Country Walks

Roger Jones
With Photographs by Duncan Skene

Ex Libris Press

First published 1983

by Roger Jones
under the imprint of

Ex Libris Press
1 The Shambles
Bradford-on-Avon
Wiltshire

Typeset by Quadraset Ltd, Radstock, Bath, Avon

Printed in Great Britain by Midway Press, Bradford-on-Avon, Wilts

ISBN 0 9506563 4 8

1st EDITION

To Hazel

Also written and published by Roger Jones:

A Book of Newton Abbot
Rambles around Newton Abbot
Where Wiltshire Meets Somerset

Written by Roger Jones and published by Countryside Books:

Wiltshire Rambles

CONTENTS

LIST OF ILLUSTRATIONS

ACKNOWLEDGEMENTS

My thanks are due to the Director of Wiltshire Library and Museum Service for permission to reproduce illustrations from works in the Headquarters Local Studies Collection in Bythesea Road, Trowbridge. I am also indebted to John Chandler, the Local Studies Officer in charge of that collection for his unfailing assistance and expert knowledge.

My thanks also to Heather and Robin Tanner for permission to quote a piece from their book *Wiltshire Village*; to the Wiltshire Archaeological and Natural History Society for permission to reproduce the portrait of William Bowles; to Rev. Davies, Rector of Beckington, for loan of a copy of William Bowles' *Sonnets and Other Poems*, which even Wiltshire Library Service could not produce; to the Kilvert Society for the photograph of Francis Kilvert; to the Moravian Book Room at Muswell Hill for permission to reproduce the portrait of John Cennick; and to all those friendly and helpful individuals I met on my rambles down the Bristol Avon.

I have consulted numerous books from libraries and from my own collection. Pevsner's Buildings of England series on the buildings of each county is indispensable. Other useful reference books are C. A. and R. A. Buchanan's volume *Industrial Archaeology of Central Southern England* (Batsford 1980), particularly for details of the Avon Navigation and Bristol City Docks. I found a good general read on Bath to be *Bath Portrait* by Bryan Little (Burleigh Press, 4th ed. 1980); the equivalent on Bristol is *Bristol, England* by H. G. Brown and P. J. Harris (Burleigh Press, rev. ed. 1979). All these are currently in print. Other works quoted are detailed in the text or in footnotes.

PREFACE

My first idea for a book on the Bristol Avon was to walk the length of the river from source to sea and simply to describe the route. The Ordnance Survey maps show there to be a right of way beside or not far from the river for almost all its 75-mile length. However, once I began walking, I found the way in some places difficult and in others less attractive and interesting than it might be. As I found out more about the towns and villages directly beside the river I was lured to other places nearby. Then it occurred to me that most people, including myself, were really more interested in completing circular walks which would constitute a good half-day's or whole-day's enjoyment. So my ideas for *Down the Bristol Avon* began to take shape: I would explore the landscape and settlements round and about the river as my reading and rambling took me, and I would explore more fully the byways which particularly interested me. Thus I devised a number of circular walks which take in the more attractive localities.

I live in Bradford-on-Avon — the object of my interest runs through the centre of this town. At Bradford the Avon forsakes the flat clay vale to cut through the same limestone massif from which, further north, it gathers its headwaters. From here the Avon follows a charming valley which also carries a railway line and the Kennet and Avon Canal. From Bradford to Avoncliff the Barton Farm Country Park stretches along the left bank of the river. After Avoncliff the valley widens to accept the River Frome, then narrows again in a majestic sweep along the famed Limpley Stoke valley before meeting the By Brook and flowing through Bath.

Often I had gazed upon the remarkable Pulteney Bridge with its narrow shops looking down onto the great stepped weir and riverside gardens. At Bristol I had been on a boat around the Floating Harbour and sensed a little of the excitement which must have characterised this handsome city when merchant ships came up the Avon and into the centre. After passing through Bristol, the Avon enters its most dramatic and impressive stretch as it flows beneath Clifton Suspension Bridge and through the unforgettable Avon Gorge. Avonmouth was familiar only from the great arch of the motorway bridge, the muddy river flowing into the Bristol Channel beneath the chimneys and sulphurous smoke of a smelting works, the dark Welsh mountains visible on the western horizon.

Upstream from Bradford-on-Avon I had seen the river as the road crosses it at Melksham, Lacock and Chippenham. I had many delights in store, especially at Malmesbury, a hill top town dominated by its half-ruined Abbey, and at Tetbury with its well-preserved townscape and Cotswoldian atmosphere. The many villages below Malmesbury are well worth exploring and, although the landscape is for the most part unspectacular, it is nevertheless full of a quiet charm which is, I suppose, partly the result of its being so unfrequented by visitors. Some of the personalities associated with this part of North Wiltshire I found most interesting. As far as I know, no one before has written up the life of John Britton, the Wiltshire antiquary of humble origin but proud ambition.

The first section of the book should act as a background to the places visited on the walks in the second section. I hope, therefore, that the book will prove enjoyable to those tackling it from an armchair as well as those using it 'in the field'. My two earlier books, *Where Wiltshire Meets Somerset* and *Wiltshire Rambles*, overlap but little with the present book. May I now invite you to join me in my rambles down the Bristol Avon. . . .

Roger Jones
Bradford-on-Avon
September 1983

1. COURSE OF THE BRISTOL AVON

WHERE does the Avon rise? If we pinpoint Malmesbury on a map we find that two streams meet just below St. John's Bridge by which we enter the town from the south. The larger of these streams is the one which enfolds Malmesbury on the south and west whilst the smaller flows by the north and east boundary. John Leland, writing about 1540, describes this as follows: 'Newton water cummith a 2 miles of the toun: and Avon water cummith by weste of the toun from Lokington a 4 miles of, and meete about a bridge at south est parte of the toun, and so goith Avon by south a while, and then turneth flat west toward Bristow.' Certainly, if we trace these streams back to their source, we find that the minor 'Newton water' flows near the village called Newnton (Newton is presumably a corruption), and is found to rise on the high ground around Tetbury. A narrow ridge north of Tetbury marks the watershed between the headwaters of the Avon and those of the Thames.

The more significant stream flowing from the west of Malmesbury rises in the grounds of Badminton Park and about Acton Turville; the various headwaters gather together near the village of Luckington (more like eight miles from Malmesbury than the four which Leland quotes). From here it flows a little north of east by Sherston and Easton Grey towards Malmesbury. Generally today and for the purposes of describing the river in this book I shall refer to the greater stream which rises to the west of Sherston as the Sherston Avon, and the lesser stream which rises about Tetbury as the Tetbury Avon.

The Sherston and Tetbury branches rise in Gloucestershire and meet in Wiltshire. More difficult to establish than the source of the Rivon Avon is the boundary of the Cotswold Hills. On the west side this is clearly defined by a steep escarpment which plunges from the highest points of the hill range to the Vale of Severn. On the east side the Cotswolds dip gently to meet the clay vale of North Wiltshire and Oxfordshire. To understand the reason for this it is necessary to know something of the geological structure of these uplands. The main component of the Cotswolds is a thick layer of limestone which is relatively hard and not easily eroded. This limestone has subsequently been raised by earth movements so that it is tilted from west to east. The effects of weathering have produced the characteristic steeply sloping scarp to the west and gently dipping slope to the east. The Cotswold limestone is overlain by other strata which have been worn away in the vicinity of the Cotswold ridge but which outcrop at the surface as we move progressively east. This is shown in diagrammatic form as follows:

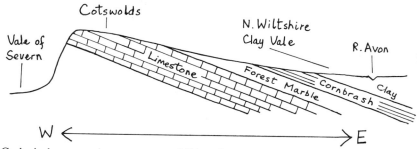

Geological cross section near source of River Avon

Not surprisingly, the drainage pattern of the Cotswolds generally follows the lie of the land which, in turn, is determined by the inclination, or dip, of the underlying strata. The Sherston Avon, in particular, is a good example of a dip stream, or consequent stream, since its direction is a consequence of the inclination of the rocks over which it flows. This branch of the Avon follows a well defined, though not deep, valley which is relatively well wooded and along which there is certainly a concentration of settlements, the inhabitants of which were assured of a ready water supply from the river itself.

Below Malmesbury the River Avon reaches the clay vale of North Wiltshire and, although taking twists and turns in almost every direction, maintains a southerly course overall. Along a line running north–south between Malmesbury and Chippenham, the gently dipping Cotswold uplands disappear beneath the clay over which the Avon flows between these two towns. The eastern boundary of the clay vale here is marked by the low hills on which Bradenstoke and Bremhill are situated. These hills owe their existence to an outcrop of the Corallian, a formation comprised of (coral) limestone and sandstone. These are relatively hard and less easily eroded than the Oxford Clay of the Avon Valley and the Kimmeridge Clay further east, and thus form a prominent feature in the landscape hereabouts. The Corallian ridge is like the Cotswold range in miniature: the west-facing scarp is steep in comparison to the eastern flank which dips more gently. From Bremhill you can see across the valley in which Calne is situated towards the hills of Bowood and the Marlborough Downs, the latter composed of chalk.

Below Chippenham the clay vale narrows, until the Avon flows through a narrow neck of land east of Lacock. The hills to the east are composed of the Lower Greensand which here, confusingly, is of a deep red colour. Further south, where the Semington Brook joins the Avon from the east, and again at Staverton near Bradford-on-Avon, the river takes a turn to the west until

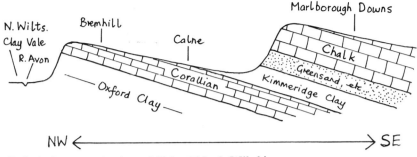

Geological cross section beyond Vale of North Wiltshire

it meets, once again, the gently sloping limestone strata from which the Cotswolds are formed. From Bradford on Avon its course is by a steep and narrow valley through the limestone plateau towards Bath. The hills are built of near horizontal strata, the upper sections of which are composed of the famous Bath Stone, i.e. the Great Oolitic Limestone, which can reach a thickness of over 100 feet. These hills have been quarried and mined since the first half of the eighteenth century when Ralph Allen acquired mineral rights on Combe Down and Bathampton Down. Bathford Hill to the east has also been extensively mined. Today stone is worked underground at Westwood and Limpley Stoke.

From Bath the Avon meanders through softer, clayey rocks but cuts a gorge through the hard sandstone about Hanham. This is the Pennant Sandstone of the Coal Measures and is a favourite building stone in and around Bristol. The valley opens out once more to carry the river through Bristol but makes a deep gorge in the Mountain Limestone below Clifton. This seems rather perverse of the Avon since it could have taken a much easier course by way of the Ashton Valley just to the south. The reason why the Avon has cut these steep valleys, first between Bradford and Bath, then at Hanham and finally and most spectacularly below Clifton and Durdham Down, is that the course of the river has been superimposed on the present landscape.

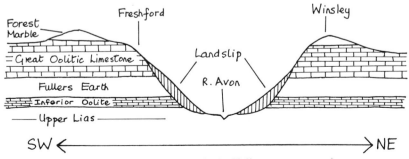

Geological cross section through Limpley Stoke Valley

Formerly, the mainly limestone strata which comprise the present range of hills we call the Cotswolds extended much farther west and south — this is shown by the existence of detached remnants, or outliers, of the same formation, like Dundry Hill south of Bristol. The whole area was uplifted, probably by several hundred feet, during earth movements in the past, and the Avon, among other rivers, was thus given greater power to cut down into its bed and carve out deep valleys. The Cotswold limestone has been stripped away around the Avon Gorge so that the river is superimposed upon a more ancient landscape.

The rocks of the Avon Gorge are much older than those encountered elsewhere along the river's course and their structure is much more complicated. From Clifton Down or from the towpath below Clifton Bridge you can see that the strata are dipping steeply — the angle of dip is about 30° to the south-east. The whole formation represents the much eroded southern limb of a great upward fold in these strata. The Mountain, or Carboniferous, Limestone is overlain by Millstone Grit and passes down into the Old Red Sandstone below Shirehampton.

All this serves to explain why the Bristol Avon is such a fascinating river: its direction follows just about every point of the compass at one place or another and the geological formations and landscape through which and beside which it flows are amazingly diverse. From the fields enclosed by dry stone walls on the Cotswold slopes to the hedged meadows of the clay vale and to the more sophisticated scenery about Bradford, Bath and Bristol — all this is found along the 75-mile course of the Bristol Avon.

I am always fascinated by descriptions of places seen through the eyes of travellers in the past, and I should like to include here an account of the Bristol Avon from source to sea which appeared in William Matthews' *New History of Bristol* published in 1794. This account was written after the construction of the Avon Navigation from Bath to Bristol and before the Floating Harbour at Bristol. The remarks regarding the convenience of Bristol Docks at this time must be taken as an acute case of guide-book writer's optimism. The long-needed Floating Harbour was begun only ten years after this guide was published. William Matthews writes as follows:

'The River Avon, tho inferior in breadth to the Thames, is one of the most notable, useful, and curious Rivers in England. As the Thames hath on its banks the two finest cities of the East, London and Oxford, so the Avon hath on hers, the two best and largest cities of the West: Bristol, the capital Key and great Mart of this country, and Bath, the most elegant City in the Kingdom, without exception. This River rises in the northern limit of Wiltshire, and runs on to the west of Breden Forest to Malmesbury, where it receives another Stream, which rises at Tetbury in Gloucestershire, and nearly encircles the place; from thence to Dantsey, 6 miles from which it receives a Stream that runs through Calne, and grows considerable on to Chippenham, where it hath a Bridge of sixteen arches over it: from thence it flows to Melksham; and having received a River that rises near the Devizes, and a Brook called Barons Brook: thus increased, goes through the middle of

Bristol from St. Augustine's Quay, 1830

Bradford under a Bridge of Eight arches. . . . From Bradford it leaves Wilts and enters Somerset; then receiving the Froom from Froom-Selwood and another rivulet comes towards Bath. Here it runs through a fruitful Vale bounded on each side by lofty and magnificent Hills, from whence the subjacent prospect of the Country, the serpentine River, the fair, beautiful buildings of Bath and its sublime and venerable Cathedral are quite enchanting. Here it runs under two elegant Bridges, the first has three equal arches, with small shops and houses on it, handsomely constructed; and the other, has five arches with a Ballustrade of Stone on each side.

'On the western side of this Bridge is the Quay of Bath, from whence the River is navigable to Bristol, so that Bath is a proper inland Port. Barges that have one mast and sail, and carry from 60 to 80 Tons, bring heavy goods from Bristol, iron, copper, wine, deals and many other articles, and generally return laden with large blocks of Freestone, the use of which is increasing here. The River, though quite fresh, is deep, of a good width, beautifully winds on towards Bristol, in an exquisitely delightful and happy Vale, between verdant hills and rural villages; and swarms with fine fishes, trout, roche, dace, perch, eels and others: about 2 miles and a half from Bath, it runs under a noble Bridge of Stone of one arch, that for height and expansion seems to rival the Rialto at Venice. A little farther on, is a lofty eminence, beautifully impending over its northern banks, on which are pleasantly situated, the elegant Mansion and Park of Sir Caesar Hawkins, Bart. Seven miles from Bristol, between Saltford and Bitton, it becomes the boundary between Gloucestershire and Somerset, and so continues till it falls into the Bristol Channel. On the eastern side of the town of Keynsham, it receives the River Chew, over which is a Bridge on the Bath road; and below the Bridge are considerable mills and manufactories for copper. Keynsham Bridge has nine arches over Avon, and near it is a lock to facilitate the navigation to Bath: at the highest tides, the salt Sea flows up to this Town. At Brislington, Avon receives another Stream, and flowing on by two works for smelting copper at Crews-hole, it enters the eastern suburbs of Bristol, between glass-houses, iron-foundries, distilleries, breweries, and sugar-houses; goes on to the City, and runs under its last and most eminent Bridge. Here, the Avon is clear and shallow at low water, deep and muddy at high water, but one of the deepest, safest, and most convenient for Navigation, in England. It is 200 feet wide at the Bridge, at high Tides rises from 25 to 30 feet perpendicularly; (exceeding the Thames in depth, which seldom rises more than 15 feet), often overflows the Key; has an agreeable effect when full, renders the port very pleasant, and will waft the largest Merchant Ships and even Ships of War up to the Bridge in the heart of the City. This River has large banks of mud down to its mouth; in the soft beds of which Ships lie securely at low water: and it yields some salmon, shads, plaice, flounders, sand dabs, plenty of eels and immense quantities of elvers.'

2. PLACES OF THE UPPER AVON:

Sherston, Tetbury, Malmesbury and villages

Where do the Cotswolds begin? This was the question I put to an old man in the pub at Pinkney which overlooks the River Avon just downstream from Sherston. 'Arh! . . . the Cotswolds be where the Avon rises, that's up around Didmarton and Badminton and Sopworth. They be over the border in Gloucestershire. This 'ere's Wiltshire.' Nor would my aged companion have it that Sherston was in the Cotswolds, presumably because this village is in Wiltshire.

Sherston looks to my foreign eye as though it belongs to the Cotswolds. It is a sizable village and has one of those wide main streets which once served as the Chipping, or market place — Sherston acquired borough status in the fifteenth century. The village is very well preserved and the High Street boasts many fine and interesting houses of the sixteenth, seventeenth and eighteenth centuries: gables and mullioned windows stand side by side with hooded doorways and tall Georgian windows.

The Church of the Holy Cross at the eastern end of the village is a splendid building representing many periods. The tall crossing tower (1730 Gothic) will impress you as you approach the entrance porch and then, as you enter the church, you will surely admire the beautiful and robust Norman arcade. The circular piers have differently decorated capitals and the round arches exhibit a characteristic zigzag moulding. The crossing arches are Early English and are adorned with some large corbel heads. The north transept contains a thirteenth-century wall tomb and is lit by a set of three lancet windows whilst the south transept has been extended to form a chapel and contains windows in the later Perpendicular style. The old winding stairway to the former rood loft is still intact.

Outside, the two-storey porch displays the strange figure known as Rattlebone, after which the pub opposite is named. Canon Jackson records that, in his day, this Rattlebone was taken by the locals to be 'the great Sherston champion, severely wounded in the fight, but heroically applying a tile-stone to his stomach to prevent his bowels gushing out'. The good Canon Jackson has his own less colourful interpretation: Rattlebone is the figure of a priest holding a book against his breast.

Sherston is built inside a fortified earthwork whose flanks slope steeply down to a stream on all sides but the east. Here it is reputed that in 1016 Edmund Ironside met and defeated the Danes under Canute and in that bloody battle the heroic Rattlebone had his finest hour. According to one source*, the old women and children of Sherston recite the following traditional verse:

> 'Fight well Rattlebone
> Thou shalt have Sherstone.'
> 'What shall I with Sherstone doe
> Without I have all belongs thereto?'
> 'Thou shalt have Wych and Wellesley,
> Easton toune and Pinkeney.'

This writer suggests that the figure known as Rattlebone may represent St. Aldhelm, Abbot of Malmesbury, whose body, he believes, passed this way on its journey to Malmesbury.

The road from Sherston to Malmesbury follows the Avon pretty closely and we may drop down to cross the river at Pinkney and Easton Grey. These are both attractive hamlets, the latter especially; here the stripling Avon curves southwards below the slopes of Easton Grey Park and the stone buildings of the village to flow beneath the old five-arched bridge. Easton Grey was the site of a station on the Roman Fosse Way; here have been excavated foundations and numerous coins. Walk 2 follows the Sherston Avon and a section of the Fosse Way.

Easton Grey, on the Sherston Avon

*Edward Hutton: *Highways and Byways in Wiltshire*, 1917.

Tetbury: Market House

Tetbury in Gloucestershire I am sure rates as a Cotswold town. Its boom time was from the medieval period to the seventeenth century, i.e. the great days of the wool trade. As that trade declined so the development of the town stabilised with the happy result that we have inherited a well-preserved, stone-built town with a certain Cotswoldian atmosphere.

The name Tetbury means 'Tette's Burg'. Tette was Abbess of Wimborne, and the earliest reference to Tetbury is a charter which shows that a monastery existed here in 681. The original settlement here is in the form of an earthwork which is distinguishable particularly on the south side of the town below the Church and above the stream. The town is mentioned in the Domesday Book as a sizeable settlement some four centuries later, and by the twelfth century there was a Cistercian monastery on the site of Estcourt Grange, just south of Tetbury. The town later developed with the wool trade and cloth industry, but, because there was an inadequate water supply so near the source of the Avon, the local merchants were unable to take advantage of power-driven machinery and the trade declined to the point of extinction in the early nineteenth century.

Tetbury has a wealth of old buildings and is well worth exploring. The Chipping is the site of the former market and is now a car park conveniently close to the centre which is dominated by the Market House, built in 1655 and supported on thick, round, stone pillars. The Market House became the centre of the town's wool trade although one end was subsequently filled in to provide a lock-up and a place to store the town's fire engine. All roads radiate from the Market House — Chipping Lane leads to the wide-open space 'The Chipping' (where there is a medieval alley including a twelfth-

21

century pointed arch) which is followed by Chipping Steps, a stepped street not accessible to cars but only to pedestrians and in the past, no doubt, to packhorses. Long Street exhibits a dazzling mixture of architectural periods and styles as does Market Place which opens out to reach a T-junction with Gumstool Hill on the left and Silver Street on the right. Church Street leads down to the exceptional church of St. Mary.

St. Mary's was originally a Norman structure but was rebuilt in Gothic style and completed in 1781 except the medieval tower and spire which were rebuilt in 1890–93. The church is best seen from the hill on the far side of the stream to the south of the town. The high and slender spire can be seen from miles away but you need to be somewhat closer to appreciate the great windows which cover the sides of the nave. These windows are really very tall and wide and were only possible given the advanced building techniques of the eighteenth century. The church is entered by a doorway from the churchyard at the north-west corner. You are presented with a passage ahead and to the left, and there are a number of doors leading off the passage in either direction. You reach the body of the church by heading straight on and bearing left under the tower. The passages around the sides of the church lead to separate entrances to the boxed pews which fill the church. I have never encountered this arrangement elsewhere; Pevsner remarks that it reminds him of the Opera House at Covent Garden, and I have read somewhere that Orthodox Christian churches are built on this pattern.

Inside you have a different but no less impressive view of those great windows which illuminate the church unusually well. The ceiling seems very high and is supported on incredibly slender columns. Pevsner says these are 'clustered columns of wood with iron cores'. The exteriors certainly fit this description, but I had the advantage of the church warden who insisted on removing the wooden skin to reveal a rough sawn circular column inside which resembled, as he said, a telegraph pole. Other items of note inside are the magnificent brass chandeliers and the gallery reminiscent of a nonconformist place of worship. We usually associate the Gothic style with the opulent decoration of the Victorian period, but here is the Gothic style of an earlier era which is elegant yet restrained.

The town really needs to be explored on foot and a useful companion to this end is the leaflet *Tetbury: a Cotswold Gem*, published by Tetbury Civic Society, which contains a number of town trails. My favourite is the circular one which follows the headwaters of the Tetbury Avon for much of its course and affords some good vantage points from which you can appreciate how the town is built in a defensive position on a hill top as well as the view of the church alluded to above.

The Sherston and Tetbury Avons unite at Malmesbury and here begins the Bristol Avon proper. Malmesbury, as we have seen, is almost entirely surrounded by the two Avons. The town is built on a ridge of Cornbrash through which the various streams have cut deep valleys to reach the underlying Forest Marble. In the words of John Leland, writing about 1540: 'The toune of Malmesbyri stondith on the very toppe of a great slaty

22

Tetbury: St. Mary's

rock, and ys wonderfully defendid by nature. . . . Newton water [Tetbury Avon] and Avon [Sherston Avon] ran so nere togither in the botom of the west suburbe at Malmesbyri, that there within a burbolt shot the toun is peninsulatid. . . . Nature hath diked the toun strongely.' The neck of land 'within a burbolt shot' is about 240 metres across and a castle once defended this position which is now occupied by the Bell Hotel adjacent to the Abbey.

The naturally defensive position of Malmesbury was utilised by the Britons as a hill-fort known as Caer Bladon, 'the Castle on the Bladon',

Malmesbury: the Abbey from the Tetbury Avon, 1894

Bladon being the river name. The *Oxford Dictionary of English Place Names* suggests that the name Malmesbury may be a compromise between 'Maldulfesburg' and 'Aldhelmesburg'. 'Maldulf' refers to Maeldub, a Celtic monk who settled here in about AD 640. The Saxons were in control of north-west Wiltshire by this time and were later led by Ine, Christian convert and king of the West Saxons. Aldhelm was Ine's kinsman and lived for a while at Maeldub's Christian settlement in Malmesbury. On his master's death in 675 Aldhelm returned to become first Abbot. Hence the town is named after its two most important early inhabitants.

Much of our knowledge of Aldhelm we owe to William of Malmesbury who was librarian and historian at the Abbey in the twelfth century where he wrote his *Life of Aldhelm* among much else. Aldhelm appears to have been an exceptionally able and energetic early Christian. Some of his own writings are extant, including a series of 101 riddles composed in Latin verse. He was indeed the first Englishman to write in Latin verse. He also wrote poetry in his native Anglo-Saxon and set it to his own music. According to one source* his concerns included censuring court ladies for waving their hair by

*Weigall, Arthur, *Wanderings in Anglo-Saxon Britain*, Hodder c. 1927.

means of curling tongs and putting too much rouge on their cheeks, and nuns for wearing beautiful dresses instead of the garb of their order. He visited the Pope in Rome whom he persuaded to place Malmesbury Abbey under direct papal jurisdiction rather than under the control of a local Bishop.

Aldhelm was made Bishop of Sherborne in 705 and travelled throughout Wessex founding churches and converting the local population to Christianity. William records that he founded the Church of St. Laurence in Bradford-on-Avon and that church remains to this day probably the most complete and best preserved Saxon church in England. It is also recorded that he founded churches at Frome and at Wareham in Dorset. He died in 709 at Doulting, near Shepton Mallet, where the village church is dedicated to him. His remains were transported back to Malmesbury to be deposited in the Abbey. He was later canonised, and Malmesbury, burial place of St. Adhelm, became a place of pilgrimage.

Aldhelm, as a Christian missionary, made quite an impact on his newly gathered flock. A delightful story is told of him that, distressed as he was by the habit of some people of leaving the church when the sermon was about to be delivered, gained the attention of the departing worshippers by positioning himself on the bridge over which they must pass on their way home and there posed as a minstrel. He would capture his audience by singing songs to the accompaniment of his harp. This done, his theme would shift from matters secular to matters spiritual and thereby he would effectively deliver his message.

The importance of Malmesbury was emphasised when King Alfred created it a borough in 880 — it is thus one of the oldest boroughs in England. King Athelstan, grandson of Alfred and first King of all England, was buried here. The men of Malmesbury helped Athelstan defeat the Danes at the decisive battle of Brunanburh in 937 and in return he presented the crown land of Malmesbury Common to the townspeople. The warring Roger Le Poer, Bishop of Sarum, surrounded Malmesbury with walls and built a castle here in the early twelth century — fragments of wall still exist and bits of the castle are incorporated into the Bell Hotel. The medieval street pattern is pretty well intact in the modern town.

The present Abbey dates from the mid-twelfth century and much splendid stonework of the Norman period remains, including the outstanding south door with its myriad carvings and the massive circular pillars of the nave. Extensive restoration was carried out in the mid-fourteenth century and a central tower was added. At 445 feet this tower was 23 feet taller than that at Salisbury; it collapsed at the end of the fifteenth century and much of the east end of the abbey went with it. What a sight Malmesbury Abbey must have been in the days when its tower was raised! Standing on its eminence above the stripling Avon, that mighty spire must have impressed itself deeply on the minds and hearts of the populace for miles around.

Following the dissolution of the monasteries in Henry VIII's reign one William Stumpe, a wealthy local clothier and M.P., purchased the Abbey and installed looms in the nave, although he later converted the former Abbey into the parish church. In the fifteenth and sixteenth centuries Malmesbury became a flourishing weaving centre, only to be left behind, like Tetbury, with the advent of power-driven machinery. Industrial activity was subsequently transferred to the production of gloves and later to lace, for which the town became renowned. Malmesbury was therefore by-passed by the industrial revolution with the happy result that we have inherited a small town which has not had its hill-top situation submerged by development beyond its river boundaries.

To my mind Malmesbury does not feel part of the Cotswolds in the way that Tetbury and Sherston do, but it is nevertheless a fascinating place, not

Malmesbury: Market Cross, 1801

least on account of the Abbey, still serving the town as parish church. Another exceptional object is the market cross dating from about 1500 at the top of the High Street. Leland describes it thus: 'There is a right fair and costely peace of worke in the Market-place made al of stone, and curiously voutid for poore market folkes to stande dry when rayne cummith.'

The Malmesbury Civic Trust publish a series of leaflets describing walks around the town and these are obtainable from Batstone Books opposite the Abbey or from the Athelstan Museum in Cross Hayes.

The country between Tetbury and Malmesbury appears roughly as a plateau through which the two young Avons have cut quite sharp valleys.

Malmesbury: a hill top town

Brokenborough is a small village situated, like Tetbury and Malmesbury, on a spur overlooking the Avon. Its church is dedicated to St. John the Baptist; the most striking feature inside is the north arcade comprising four bays supported by three circular and massive but alarmingly tilted pillars. These date from the thirteenth century, as does the chancel arch. John Aubrey, writing after the Civil War, records the following: 'In the church, before the warres, they say were very fine windows, now utterly defaced: an

27

old man told me that his Father, who dyed twenty-four years since, was 110 at his death, and remembered in the tyme of the old lawe, eighteen little bells that hung in the middle of the Church; the pulling of one wheel made them ring, which was done at the Elevation of the Hoste.'

The contrast with St. John the Baptist at Shipton Moyne could hardly be more complete — this is a splendid Victorian edifice dating from the 1860s and built in the Early English style. The interior contains many objects from the earlier church. In the chancel are three effigies — two knights in armour

Fosse Way crossing the Tetbury Avon

and a lady. In the Estcourt Chapel is a canopied monument with effigies of Judge Estcourt (died 1600) and his wife, both in full Elizabethan costume. Close by is a second and more elaborate canopied monument in Renaissance style dating from 1624. Estcourts have been interred here since 1325. The list of rectors dates from 1297 and it is notable that two rectors put in a total of 104 years — from 1806 to 1910 — in the service of this parish.

The Fosse Way slices through north-west Wiltshire to form the line of many parish boundaries as well as a stretch of the county boundary itself. The conquering Romans built the Fosse Way as a frontier and as a line of communication along which military forces could be directed to quell the troublesome British. Walk 1 follows the Roman road for a short distance and reaches its crossing point over the Avon.

3. MALMESBURY TO CHIPPENHAM

Below Malmesbury the valley of the Avon gradually opens out to reach the clay vale. The M4 cuts through the county from east to west and is about equidistant from both towns. For the rambler the motorway effectively separates the Somerfords and Dauntsey to the north from Sutton Benger, Christian Malford, Kellaways and the Tythertons to the south. This is unspectacular though very pleasant country and there is much in it to interest the curious rambler. Leland writes as follows:

'Riding between Malmesbyri and Chippenham al the ground on that side of the ryver was chaumpain, fruteful of corne and grasse, but little wood. . . . Al the quarters of the foreste of Braden be welle wooddid, even along from Malmesbyri to Chippenham ward.'

The forest of Braden has today all but vanished although the slopes of the hill which rise to the remains of Bradenstoke Abbey and Lyneham Airfield appear well wooded from the Malmesbury-Chippenham road. The higher ground is good corn-growing land whilst the low-lying meadows about the Avon are best suited to cattle grazing. The clay vale was much more wooded before Dutch Elm Disease took its toll on the tall and stately elm trees which were most typical of the hedgerows hereabouts.

Little Somerford is a village some distance from the river. Its name reminds us that, in this locality, it was only possible to ford the Avon in summer when the waters were low. The village church, like that at Brokenborough and Shipton Moyne, is dedicated to St. John the Baptist. It has a plain perpendicular tower, nave, chancel and porch. You enter the church by a massive wooden door. The church's main interest lies in the objects between nave and chancel. The Perpendicular rood screen is a fine example and is reputed to have come from Malmesbury Abbey. Above the screen is a tympanum which is plastered on the nave side and decorated with the Royal Arms of Elizabeth I and dated 1602. Adjacent to the rood screen on the left is a Jacobean pulpit and reader's desk dated 1626, and on the window sill beside the pulpit is a fragment from a medieval cross which once stood in the churchyard but which was discovered under the pulpit during restoration. On one side is carved the Madonna and Child, on the other the Crucifixion.

Great Somerford, further south and on the opposite bank of the river, is built mainly on a bluff overlooking the level meads. It is also a well-spread-out village and contains some attractive buildings. The church of St. Peter and St. Paul is sited impressively at the north side of the village on a rise above the Avon and is approached by a drive from the road. Great Somerford church dates from the fourteenth century although much restored over a century ago. The interior seems particularly inviting and well-cared for and, indeed, well used. This makes up for the fact that there is little of any great historical or architectural interest. Instead we have what a parish church should be: a living place of worship and not a dusty old museum.

However, two extremely attractive features are to be seen in the chancel. One is the ceiling which is delicately and intricately painted with flowers, the other is the modern stained-glass window which commemorates the life and service of a former rector, Rev. Albert Lutley, who spent many years as a missionary in China. The modern dress of the children depicted and, even more, the two great Chinese dragons rearing up above the human figures come as quite a shock to one used to gazing at representations of the life of Christ and the Saints.

A memorial plaque in the chancel wall records the incumbency of Stephen Demainbray, who was appointed rector here in 1799. He was subsequently Chaplain to George III and superintendent of the Royal Observatory at Richmond. One of his chief concerns was the fate of peasants dispossessed by the Enclosure Acts. He improved and extended the glebe property in the village and successfully lobbied for the advantage his poorer parishioners might gain from the allotment system and, about 1830, let some of the glebe in this manner. He wrote a pamphlet *The Poor Man's Best Friend* in the hope that he might persuade owners of properties in other parishes to do likewise.

At Dauntsey, Aubrey notes that, 'Here is a stately Parke with admirable oakes: the ground too, good. The meadows and pastures here are famous at Smithfield Markett: no better fatting ground in England'. The manor house has a plain Georgian façade but the church is rather more interesting. The church of St. James is an ancient one — the oldest parts date from Norman times but a former lord of the manor, the Earl of Danby, in the seventeenth century built the tower and the north chapel and provided most of the furniture, including the boxed pews. Inside there is a useful guide which leads you around the church and gives much fascinating background to the curiosities of this building. An object I find quite stunning is the doom painting hanging on the wall at the back of the nave.

At Little Somerford we saw a tympanum above the rood loft painted with the arms of Queen Elizabeth I and this no doubt replaced an earlier doom painting the likes of which at one time decorated many such tympanums in our parish churches. After the Reformation these were decreed superstitious and destroyed or replaced by the Royal Arms to emphasise the supremacy of State over Church. But what a treasure we have here at Dauntsey, although this rare object is in a poor state of preservation. What we see is a portrayal of the Day of Judgement with naked figures in line for Heaven or Hell, the latter being thrust into the flaming jaws of a hideous monster. It puts me in mind of certain paintings by Hieronymous Bosch and one can imagine the effect on members of the congregation of this great painting hung over their heads as they stood in church.

Christian Malford: All Saints

South of the motorway the villages of Sutton Benger and Christian Malford face each other from opposite banks of the Avon. Of Sutton Benger, Aubrey notes that, 'Anciently in the parish were vineyards, which are recited among other grants to the Longs by King Henry VIII. Gravelly lands is the most natural for vines'. All Saints Church was heavily restored in the mid-nineteenth century. All Saints at Christian Malford exhibits work of varying periods and is certainly an attractive building, set in its peaceful churchyard on a slight bluff above Avon's swirling waters. Inside all is bright and airy, even the chancel beyond the rood screen.

Three abandoned lines of communication are encountered between Malmesbury and Chippenham. These include the Malmesbury and Calne branch railway lines and the Wilts and Berks Canal. Malmesbury Railway was promoted in 1871 and incorporated in1872 to make a 6½-mile branch from Dauntsey. The Great Western Railway worked the line from its inception in 1877 and a goods depot was added to the intermediate station at Somerford two years later. As an economy the branch line was shortened by the abandonment of the Dauntsey-Kingsmead Mill level-crossing section and a short spur was laid to connect with the main line at Little Somerford. Passenger services were withdrawn in 1951, well before the Beeching axe fell, and goods traffic ceased soon after.

The Calne Railway was the first in Wiltshire built as a local venture to serve local needs — more than half the capital needed was subscribed by the Harris family of Calne whose business interests stood to improve. The 5¾-mile stretch of broad-gauge line from Chippenham to Calne was opened in 1863. From the outset it was worked by the G.W.R. C. R. Clinker, in his account of the branch line written before closure for the Victoria County History, says, 'The branch conveys a considerable amount of parcels and goods traffic, and some 2,000 vans of parcels, mainly bacon, sausages and cooked meats are dispatched annually to all parts of the country.' Goods traffic ceased in 1964, passenger traffic in the following year and, incidentally, the Harris Bacon Company of Calne closed down in 1983.

The Wilts and Berks Canal was built under an Act of Parliament of 1795 from Semington on the Kennet and Avon Canal to Abingdon on the Thames in Oxfordshire. The canal therefore formed a link between the Bristol Avon and the River Thames although it was never used as a through route but rather for local traffic between the Somerset Coalfield and the Vale of the White Horse. Local branches were built to serve both Chippenham and Calne. The Wilts and Berks enjoyed only a modest prosperity and was all but disused by 1900.

Five walks are described in the country between Malmesbury and Chippenham (Walks 3–7). I have devoted the following three chapters to objects encountered and personalities associated with the villages of this district. The village churches south of the M4 are not especially interesting, but particularly attractive is the little Early English church of St. Nicholas at West Tytherton which enjoys a peaceful situation, having only farmhouses and open fields for company. St. Peter's Church in Langley Burrell has a special magic too — it may be something to do with its association with Francis Kilvert, the love and devotion with which he ministered to his parishioners and the fact that it is now regularly frequented by readers of *Kilvert's Diary*. Certainly the church has a warm and cared-for atmosphere and sits prettily in its tree-lined churchyard.

West Tytherton: St. Nicholas

I especially enjoyed the walking in the country between the motorway and Chippenham. The peaceful Avon meads traversed by Maud Heath's Causeway and dotted with ancient farmhouses are alluring — so too are the slopes of Wick Hill to the east which lead to the delightful village of Bremhill, and the rising land to the west with the villages of Langley Burrell, Kington Langley, Draycot and Kington St. Michael with their many historical and literary associations. The community which Heather and Robin Tanner describe with such well-chosen words and finely executed drawings and etchings in their book *Wiltshire Village* is a composite of these places. Written in the days before Dutch Elm Disease, the opening paragraph describes the setting of the quasi fictional village of Kington Borel as follows:

'All the land between the village and the downs looks almost like the forest it once was, so richly timbered is it, for apart from the woods and copses themselves there is hardly a field that is not hedged by heavy elms. All day the Avon lies hidden, but at dawn the course can be traced by the white mist that hangs above it.'

4. TWO LOCAL CLERGYMEN:

William Bowles and Francis Kilvert

The country parson is an enduring figure in English life and letters and two interesting but quite different individuals served nearby parishes between Malmesbury and Chippenham. William Bowles was rector of Bremhill in the first half of the last century and Francis Kilvert curate at Langley Burrell in the latter half.

William Bowles William Lisle Bowles became vicar of Bremhill in 1804 and remained so for nearly half a century. The *Oxford Companion to English Literature* says that he is chiefly remembered for his *Fourteen Sonnets* published in 1789, 'the first of any merit that had appeared for a long period'. By 1805 Bowles' Sonnets had run to nine editions. Coleridge was so impressed that he wrote out forty copies to give to his friends. Southey, Wordsworth and Charles Lamb were among others who admired the Sonnets of William Bowles, though he never produced anything as good again. Nor did he attract the same attention by anything he wrote, except perhaps by a controversial edition of Pope which appeared in 1806 and which was followed by a series of leaflets attacking Pope and the value of his poetry. William Bowles had a reputation as a great individualist, not to say eccentric, and I would like to give a brief account of the man who ministered to Bremhill for so many years and lived in the parsonage which commands such a fine prospect across the valleys of the Marden and Avon.

In 1769, at the age of six, William Bowles moved with his family from Northamptonshire to Somerset, where his clergyman father had been promoted to the living of Uphill and Brean. At Winchester, young William developed a love of nature, the ancient classics and Shakespeare and Milton. From Winchester he went up to Trinity College. After a broken engagement, William sought solace in travel and visited the North of England, Scotland, the Rhine and Switzerland. It was on his Rhine trip that he began writing sonnets and it was then that his best poetry was written. He returned to England when, in need of money, he entered into an arrangement with Richard Cruttwell, a Bath printer, to produce one hundred copies of his *Fourteen Sonnets*. A second edition of five hundred copies followed the same year and many subsequent editions appeared in following years, to which he added later poems.

The fourth edition of 1796 includes a longish poem entitled *Elegy, written at*

William Bowles

the Hotwells, Bristol in July 1789. This is a lament for a lost friend, Rev. Thomas Russel, a fellow poet who had died at Hotwells the previous year. This poem was evidently composed as William Bowles sat on Clifton Down watching the sun rise over the Avon Gorge. Bowles' words may sound a little 'over the top' to modern ears but he quite obviously found much to inspire him in the world of nature and in many ways presaged the naturalistic movement of the following century. I thought it worth quoting a part of this poem as an example of Bowles' work and because it describes a memorable length of the Bristol Avon. The first four stanzas are as follows:

> The morning wakes in shadowy mantle grey,
>   The darksome woods their glimmering skirts unfold,
> Prone from the cliff the falcon wheels her way,
>   And long and loud the bell's slow chime is toll'd.

The redd'ning light gains fast upon the skies,
  And far way the glist'ning vapours sail,
Down the rough steep th'accustom'd hedger hies,
  And the stream winds in brightness thro' the vale!

How beauteous the pale rocks above the shore
  Uplift their bleak and furrow'd aspect high;
How proudly desolate their foreheads hoar,
  That meet the earliest sunbeam of the sky!

Bound to yon dusky mart, with pennants gay,
  The tall bark, on the winding water's line,
Between the riven cliffs plies her hard way,
  And peering on the sight the white sails shine.

After regretting those in bad health and those who have passed away,
particularly his former friend Thomas Russel, Bowles ends refreshed and
optimistic, thanks to the beauty of his surroundings:

Thankful, that still the landscape beaming bright,
  Of pendant mountain, or of woodland gray,
Can wake the wonted sense of pure delight,
  And charm awhile my solitary way!

Enough: Through the high heavens the proud sun rides,
  My wand'ring steps their silent path pursue
Back to the crouded world where fortune guides:
  CLIFTON, to thy white rocks and woods adieu!

In 1788 Bowles was ordained deacon to the curacy of Knoyle in south-
west Wiltshire. Four years later he was engaged to the rector's daughter but
her father objected to their proposed marriage and she died in 1793. In 1797
he married Magdalen Wake, sister of his former fiancée. It is unclear
whether the rector had a change of heart or whether he, too, had died but
Magdalen and William were soon married and lived happily together until
her death nearly fifty years later.

William Bowles eventually secured the living at Bremhill in 1804 and this
position brought him every advantage he sought: an ample salary and a
beautiful rural situation. He was near many Wiltshire antiquities such as
Avebury and the Wansdyke and he devoted much time to their study and to
the development of (usually) wild theories concerning the same. Bowles was
also very near Bowood and he frequently enjoyed the company of its many
distinguished visitors.

He began re-styling his parsonage in conformity with his own ideas of
architecture and garden design. In his book, *History of Bremhill*, published in
1828, Bowles maintains that a parsonage should be unobtrusive and should
harmonise with the church. He writes (in the third person): 'In the
parsonage house of his parish, the ideas of consonance and picturesque
propriety have been consulted, as far as they could be adopted, the house

being old, but large and convenient. By parapetting the whole with a simple gothic ornamental railing, such as appears on the church at Stourhead, a unity has been given to the exterior, and the long low roofs have put on an ecclesiastical appearance.' The reader can judge the result of Bowles' alterations from the accompanying engraving, made from a drawing presented to John Britton by Bowles for inclusion in the third volume of his *Beauties of Wiltshire*.

Bremhill Parsonage, 1825

Southey thought Bremhill 'a perfect paradise of a place' but Bowles' neighbour Tom Moore, who lived at nearby Bromham, wrote in his diary in 1818 that, 'Bowles parsonage house at Bremhill is beautifully situated; but he has frittered away its beauty with grottos, hermitages, and Shenstonian inscriptions'. Notwithstanding the time Bowles spent on his house and garden and various writings he also showed great interest in his parishioners, in the education of the children of the poor and in his choir. The parson was beloved by his flock which increased in size during his incumbency. In 1828 Bowles was appointed canon of Salisbury Cathedral and thereafter spent three winter months each year in Salisbury where he delighted in his duties with the cathedal's music, for music was another of his many talents and enthusiasms. He was grief-stricken when his wife died in 1844. He resigned his duties at Bremhill and retired to Salisbury where he spent the last five years of his life.

William Bowles was a man of contradictions. He was at once talented, cultured, dedicated to the service of his fellows but at the same time remarkably simple, credulous — a true innocent. It was surely the childlike side of his nature which endeared him to his many influential friends. Above all he was a great eccentric and had a reputation for absent-mindedness. When dressing for dinner once his wife found him in a terrible state because

37

Bremhill: St. Martin's

a silk stocking had unaccountably disappeared, until at length he realised he had put both stockings on one leg. During a trip on horseback he dismounted to walk down a steep hill, forgot to remount and so walked along the turnpike with the reins over his arm until he reached the gate, where his offer to pay the toll brought him to his senses and the discovery that his horse had slipped the bridle and disappeared. Perhaps the best story is the most quoted one of his attending a school prize giving — he handed a child a copy of the Bible in which he had inscribed 'With the Author's Compliments'. His irrational fears led him at one period to live in such dread of rabid dogs that he went around wearing heavy-duty overalls to prevent his being bitten. He is also said to have measured the distance between his prebendal house and Salisbury Cathedral to ascertain whether he would be in danger if the spire should fall.

Let us leave it to his friend Robert Southey to have the last word on William Bowles: 'He has indulged his natural timidity to a degree little short of insanity, yet he laughs, himself, at follies which he is nevertheless continually committing. He is literally afraid of everything. His oddity, his untidyness, his simplicity, his benevolence, his fear, and his good nature, make him one of the most extraordinary characters I ever met with.'

Francis Kilvert   Francis Kilvert and his famous diary are primarily associated with the border country of Radnorshire and Herefordshire where the clergyman served as curate for seven years and as vicar for the last three years of his life. It is this area which is usually referred to as 'Kilvert Country'. There is another Kilvert Country, however, and that is the parish of Langley Burrell near Chippenham, where Francis assisted his rector father as curate during 1863–64 and again from 1872–76.

Francis Kilvert was born at Hardenhuish in 1840 where his father, Robert Kilvert, was Rector. He and his five brothers and sisters were educated, with other pupils their father engaged, at Hardenhuish, but later Francis was sent to his uncle's school at Claverton Lodge, in the village of that name which overlooks the Avon between Bradford and Bath. Kilvert's mother was the daughter of Squire Coleman of Kington St. Michael and his wife, Thermuthis, daughter of the Ashe family, squires of Langley Burrell. Robert Ashe was both squire and parson of Langley Burrell and his son, Robert Martin Ashe, took holy orders and assisted his father as curate. When the rector died his son resigned his clerical duties and concentrated his efforts on running the estate. Thus it was that in 1855, when Francis Kilvert was fifteen and still at school in Bath, his father Robert Kilvert was appointed to the living at Langley Burrell.

In 1859 Squire Ashe demolished the old rectory which stood close by the church and moved Robert Kilvert and his family into the spacious, mainly eighteenth-century house just south of the village and now known as Kilvert's Parsonage. This is a private house which can be seen amid trees across the fields from the main road from Chippenham to Langley Burrell. Squire Ashe's manor house remained near the church but the removal of the old rectory and several cottages towards the village served to clear his view.

Francis Kilvert completed his education at Oxford and took holy orders in 1863. Now he returned to Langley Burrell to assist his father as curate. Of his diary only a small part has survived. His wife destroyed much of it for personal reasons and an elderly niece destroyed all but three of the twenty-two surviving notebooks when she inherited them from her brother. The present diary was published in three volumes between 1938 and 1940 and is still in print. A selected edition is available in Penguin, the cover of which bears a still from the B.B.C. television series *Kilvert's Diary*. The diary we have inherited begins in 1870 and ends in 1879, the year of Kilvert's death.

Kilvert's Diary was one of those books which I had always intended to read but had never quite got around to doing so. It was the connection with Langley Burrell and my rambles along the Avon which prompted me to begin reading. What a delightful and rewarding experience it is to enter the world of the Rev. Francis Kilvert through the pages of his diary! Langley Burrell and all its inhabitants, of high rank and low, are lovingly portrayed. The descriptive passages are remarkably fresh and vivid, often moving, and the whole gives a rich insight into a rural Wiltshire community of a century ago.

On Monday 16th May, 1870, Kilvert left Clyro in Radnorshire to pay a visit to Langley Burrell. He writes as follows: 'Got to Chippenham shortly before 2 p.m. I walked up by Cocklebury, the lane and fields deliciously shady green and quiet. My father came across the Common to the black gate waiting for me by that way, then came over the field to meet me. The orchard and garden apple trees are in full bloom and the pink stage of the blossom having passed, the trees seem loaded as if with snow, a sea, a mass of blossom. The copper beech is in its early purple splendour and the great laburnum near it just about to burst into blossom. The broom that I transplanted has grown much and is in fine bloom now. The whole place is looking almost more lovely than ever I saw it, and the grass of the lawn so smooth and brilliantly green.'

On Wednesday he went by train to the Bath Flower Show, on Thursday he had a bad face ache, and on Sunday, 'We all went to church this morning except Dora, walking together as one great family through the may, between the hawthorn hedges and trees laden with sweet snowy blossom. The Bowling green, Becks and the Barrow meadow are sheets of golden buttercups, seas of gold stretching away under the elms. In Becks there are scarlet may trees and the deep blue sky over all'.

The following week Kilvert records fishing in the Avon, going for an early morning walk 'along the Common on Maud Heath between the may hedges', and a visit to Monkton Farleigh, near Bradford-on-Avon, to attend a croquet and archery party. And so the diary continues, revealing the day-to-day activities, relationships and personal feelings of a country parson who faithfully attended to his flock and took delight in the people and the natural world around him.

Many local names crop up again and again in the pages of Kilvert's Diary, such as Peckingell, Rawlings, Cocklebury, Kellaways, Kington St. Michael and Draycot, all of which he visited regularly. Bowood, that pinnacle of the Chippenham social scene, was, however, beyond the aspirations of a lowly country parson and it remained unvisited by Kilvert. He relates the story of the long-standing feud between the men of Langley Burrell and those of Chippenham which led to pitched battles and even to deaths. In the end the Langley Burrell men put flight to a mob of Chippenham men, even though the former were outnumbered five-to-one. Kilvert often made trips to London to visit art galleries and so on, but he was always glad to return: 'How delightful to get down into the sweet fresh damp air of the country again.'

It is usually said that Kilvert was happiest at Clyro. There is no doubt that he delighted in the hill country there and found great fulfilment in serving the inhabitants of the happy little community which Clyro appeared to have been at the time. Nevertheless, the rather less dramatic landscape of the

Francis Kilvert

middle Avon in North Wiltshire served to inspire him: 'As I walked along the field path I stopped to listen to the rustle and solemn night whisper of the wheat, so different to its voice by day. The corn seemed to be praising God and whispering its evening prayer. Across the great level meads near Chippenham came the martial music of a drum and fife band, and laughing voices of unseen girls were wafted from farms and hayfields out of the wide dusk'.

At other points in the diary it is clear that in this place Kilvert sensed a certain tension in society. He often chides those in authority for their thoughlessness and unkindness towards those less fortunate; at times he expresses feelings of anger and frustration. He strikes an uncharacteristically negative note on 28th October 1874 when, faced with Squire Ashe's determination that the leader of the church choir be dismissed and that the church should not have a harmonium, Kilvert writes that 'We are prepared to give up the living and leave the place should we be obliged to do so rather than submit any longer to this tyranny. . . . We should all be better and happier elsewhere, more independent, and what is most important of all we should have more self-respect. For my own part I should for many reasons be glad and thankful to go. I don't know how it will end. I suppose I shall stay here as long as my Father lives, no longer'.

In 1876 he was presented with a living in Radnorshire and in 1877 with one in Herefordshire. He married in August 1879 and died suddenly one month after, at the age of 38 years.

I first encountered Francis Kilvert in my rambles beside the Avon and I would like to quote, in conclusion, a lovely passage from his diary in which he expresses ideas about walking along footpaths which I have long felt: 'I love to wander on these soft gentle mournful autumn days, alone among the quiet peaceful solitary meadows, tracing out the ancient footpaths and mossy overgrown stiles between farm and hamlet, village and town, musing of the many feet that have trodden these ancient and now well nigh deserted and almost forgotten ways and walking in the footsteps of the generations that have gone before and passed away.'

Langley Burrell: St. Peter's

5. TWO LOCAL ANTIQUARIES:

John Aubrey and John Britton

Though both antiquaries of some note John Aubrey and John Britton exhibit a marked contrast in the style and content of their work. Aubrey appears to be strong on inspiration and weak on method whilst Britton is quite the reverse. John Aubrey lived in the seventeenth century and is well known. John Britton wrote and published his works during the first half of the last century and is comparatively unknown. For this reason I have devoted more of this chapter to an account of John Britton.

John Aubrey was born in 1626 at Easton Pierse in the parish of Kington St. Michael. He was educated locally, at Blandford in Dorset, at Oxford and at the Middle Temple, though he did not complete his education at the last two places. He inherited the family estate in Wiltshire at the age of 26 and during the 1650s and 60s enjoyed the life of a country gentleman but all the time fighting a losing battle with his father's debtors. A series of lawsuits bankrupted him by the 1670s and he spent the rest of his life as an itinerant scholar, relying for bodily support on the hospitality of his friends and pursuing the many and varied interests which obsessed him. He was, indeed, at some point in his life interested in nearly everything. He wrote copiously and is perhaps best-known as a biographer through his book *Brief Lives*, but also as an antiquary in his 'discovery' of Avebury in his *Wiltshire Topographical Collections* which were edited by Canon Jackson of Leigh Delamere and published by the Wiltshire Archaeological and Natural History Society in 1862, and as a scientist in his *Natural History of Wiltshire*, which was edited by John Britton and published in 1847. The only one of Aubrey's works published in his own lifetime was *Miscellanies*, a collection of superstitions and strange happenings.

Much of Aubrey's jumbled writings remain in manuscript form. A recent biographer of Aubrey is Michael Hunter and in his book *John Aubrey and the Realm of Learning* (Duckworth 1975) he expresses the view that much of Aubrey's contribution to the development of scientific ideas has been underrated, indeed largely ignored, and his book sets out to redress the balance. His social activities are most entertainingly described in the book *John Aubrey and His Friends* (Constable 1946) by Anthony Powell. John Aubrey's contemporary, Anthony Wood, described him as 'maggotty

John Aubrey

headed, and sometimes little better than crazed. And being exceedingly credulous would stuff his many letters to Anthony Wood with fooleries and misinformations, which sometimes would guide him into the paths of error'.

In gathering material for his Wiltshire studies, Aubrey visited all the parish churches in Wiltshire and, wherever possible, talked to the local gentry. From this source he acquired information which he did not usually bother to check. The many queries and memoranda which appear in his notes were intended to catch the attention of his brother William who remained at Kington St. Michael and was supposed to seek answers to these myriad questions of John's. Aubrey's writings on Wiltshire are sometimes less informative than entertaining. Perhaps it will help us to judge his work by quoting a sample, viz. the description of Bradford-on-Avon which appears in *The Topographical Collections*:

'This is a Market Towne; market day . . .

At the end of the great barne is a hand holding a battle ax, which is the crest of Hall.

I would have the prospect taken of Mr. J. Hall's howse which is very fine. In this Towne is a fair old built howse of the family of Rogers of Cannington, here are many old escutcheons, which see; now it is the seat of Mr. Methwyn, the Cloathier.

On the top of the North Hill, above Mr. Methwyn's, is the finest hermitage I have seen in England; severall roomes and a very neate chapell of good freestone. This high hill is rock and gravel, faces the south and southwest, therefore is the best seate for a vineyard of any place I know; better in England cannot be.

Mr. Thomas Gore assures me that in the Church here, is nothing of antiquitie to be found.

Here is a strong and handsome bridge in the middest of which is a little chapell, as at Bathe, for Masse. *Mem.* A little beyond the bridge is a chapell and almshouse of an old date. *Q.* Whose donacion?'

The editor of this work, Canon Jackson, refers the reader to Rev. Jones' *History of Bradford*. In this instance, Aubrey's description is dated rather than inaccurate although Jackson says of Barton Farm it is doubtful whether the crest of Hall was ever there, and one wonders if Aubrey visited Holy Trinity Church himself when he assures the reader that it contained nothing of antiquity!

Bradford-on-Avon: The Hall

45

John Britton   John Britton was born in the village of Kington St. Michael, near Chippenham, in 1771. *Beauties of Wiltshire* was Britton's first topographical work, the first two volumes of which were published in 1801. The third and final volume dealing with his native North Wiltshire did not appear until 1826, and included a brief memoir of the author. This was followed by a three-part autobiography published in 1850. We therefore know much of Britton's background and subsequent career.

John Britton's father was baker, maltster, shopkeeper and small farmer in Kington St. Michael. He describes his house as 'rather better than most' with whitewashed walls and thatched roof. The internal and external finishing was 'rude and simple'. He says 'one room served for kitchen and parlour and hall. It was about fourteen feet square, by six feet and a half high; with a large beam beneath the ceiling, attached to which was a bacon-rack which served to hold two flitches, with a gun, sticks, whips, and other articles. The floor consisted of irregular slabs of stone, not greater than an inch in thickness. . . . The shop was about the same size as this room and communicated with it'.

John Britton's childhood home

It was John Britton's mother who successfully managed the shop and the business side of the family's affairs. As the number of children increased, Mrs. Britton spent more time attending to her growing family and less to the shop and business. Her husband could not cope and the result was ruin. In John Britton's words: 'Mother died broken-hearted and father became idiotic'. Of the surviving seven children, five, including John, were sent to London to seek their fortune. Before we accompany young John to London, let us first discover him as a child in his native village.

In his autobiography he records that, 'From my earliest remembrances, I was ever active, inquisitive, emulous, ambitious, and sensitive; whether at play, at school, or at work. It was my constant aim to surpass my equals, and compete with my superiors'. It would perhaps be unfair to accuse John Britton of considering himself too good for his fellows but he was certainly very critical of the shortcomings of his native village which he describes as 'rude and truly illiterate'. He observes the 'absence of all moral and legal authority in the parish', and that 'without a regular clergyman to advise and admonish, or a magistrate, or private gentleman residing in the principal house of the village the inhabitants were undisciplined, illiterate, and deprived of all good example'.

He contrasts his perception of Kington St. Michael with that of Miss Mitford in her book *Our Village*, which describes, with great affection, the village of Three Mile Cross, near Reading, as being 'full of innocence, cheerfulness and social happiness' This is too much for John Britton, who maintains that 'Many poets and essayists have eulogised rustic life and manners, as being replete with sylvan joys — arcadian scenes — primeval innocence — and unsophisticated pleasures'. He admonishes them: 'Alas! these are but the closet dreams of metropolitan poets and visionary enthusiasts; for I fear that all their pleasing pictures are wholly drawn from imagination, and not from nature. . . . Genuine rustics have very little more sagacity than the brutes with whom they associate'. In this context it is easy to guess into which category Britton would place G. Shepherd, the painter of this view of Kington St. Michael in 1824.

Kington St. Michael, 1824

Kington St. Michael Britton describes as 'a purely agricultural locality; there has never, in fact, been a loom in the parish. All the farms are engaged in dairying, cheese being the most important product'. All the roads to the village branched off from turnpike roads and were not easy for wheeled traffic: 'Our dull village was periodically enlivened by the visits of a clothier; with one, two, or three horses, laden with bags of wool, brought from the manufacturers in Gloucestershire and doled out to poor women, to be carded and spun for the weaver's loom. Thus several women and their daughters were employed, and derived regular payment for their labour. The ceremonies of distributing the wool, receiving and paying for the spun yarn, and supplying the poor with articles for domestic use, were transacted at our house, which was thronged on these occasions.'

Other occasional visitors to the village included the Duke of Beaufort's hunt and the doctor, 'this itinerant quack', and his clown. Thus Britton describes his village as remote, largely unfrequented by strangers and containing no persons above the rank of farmer or village tradesman. In such a place was Britton 'destined to pass many precious years without the acquisition of any practical or useful knowledge'.

Britton found some stimulus to his desire for self-improvement in an uncle who worked in the Chancery office in London and who spent the three-month-long Law vacation in the country. The impressionable young nephew visited him on these occasions and 'it was then I first imbibed the feeling of ambition — became enamoured of what appeared genteel dress, genteel manners, and refined discourse and habits, compared with the clownish deportment, the uneducated and uncouth language, and the broad, prolonged pronunciation of my village companions. Kington now lost all its charms'.

It was this uncle that arranged John's apprenticeship with a London wine merchant, which he began at the age of sixteen, and very quickly grew to hate. He learned little of the wine trade but spent his time in a wine cellar forcing and fining wines, and bottling, corking and binning the same. 'The long, dreary and cheerless period of apprenticeship, which it was my fate to endure for nearly six years, embraced a series of privations and mortifications of a most serious and depressing nature'. He was constantly ill. Books were his only escape: he records that he did much reading during his term of 'legal English slavery'. From his reading he diagnosed his illness and perhaps the knowledge alone was sufficient to prevent him becoming victim of his condition.

During his early morning walks before work he became acquainted with one Mr. Essex, a painter of watch faces, who became Britton's mentor and guide and lent and bought him books. In Mr. Essex's shop Britton was introduced to the local literati including Edward Brayley, an apprentice enameller. Britton and Brayley co-published a single ballad entitled *The Guinea Pig*, which was a great success, though most of the copies sold were a pirated edition.

At this time, too, John fell in love with the maid servant of his employer's son's new wife. When he was eventually released from his apprenticeship he

48

John Britton

set out to walk to Plympton to visit Elisabeth Bryant, his beloved 'Betsy'. On his way he returned to Wiltshire and his native village which, for once, he speaks of with happiness, even affection, after his long absence. He set out for Plympton in the autumn of 1793 with one purpose in mind and quite oblivious, he records with some regret, to the natural and architectural beauties which he passed. The eventual meeting was a disaster; Betsy's employer demanded that they end their relationship once and for all, and Betsy complied with her employer's wish. So it was that the rejected lover returned to his inn 'disconsolate, and almost deranged' and contemplating suicide.

Poor John returned to London penniless and took odd jobs here and there in order to make ends meet and to pursue his own self-improvement and, he hoped, a literary career. The former he achieved by leading an abstemious life, by reading, by attending debating societies, and the latter by writing essays and reviews for periodicals such as *Sporting Magazine*. John Wheble, printer, bookseller and publisher of this magazine, suggested that Britton should write *Beauties of Wiltshire* and advanced him some money. Britton felt unqualified to do so and it was not until he teamed up once more with Edward Brayley that the project got off the ground. The first two volumes of *Beauties of Wiltshire* were published in 1801. Thus seven years elapsed from the time of Britton's release from his apprenticeship until his adoption of literature as a profession, 'a time of vicissitudes, privations and hardships'.

After this initial success Brayley and Britton proposed a series to be known as *Beauties of England and Wales*: Bedfordshire was the first county to appear. Britton records that, 'Now we became concerned about the accuracy and originality of the information which we compiled — our topographical notes were by far too meagre for the gratification of antiquarian curiosity. Our publisher thought otherwise and urged us forward by stating that such works did not require much original matter — that there were plenty of publications to copy from and abridge'. Although Britton promised to visit all the places he described and to glean as much information as possible from the gentlemen he met, there can be no doubt that he took his publisher's advice, not to mention the absence of any original research in his work.

In the preparation of *Beauties of England and Wales*, Brayley was to cover certain counties and Britton others. Differences arose between the two men and there is little doubt that the series was not the commercial success it might have been and was never completed. Now Britton branched out to pursue his own projects, including the series *Architectural Antiquities*, which comprised four large quarto volumes containing many engravings and articles, some of which were written by friends. This series proved a success and was followed by another series *Cathedral Antiquities of England*. In addition there were many odd titles such as a work on Fonthill Abbey and an edition of John Aubrey's *National History of Wiltshire*, still in print.

The great value and attraction of John Britton's many topographical works must surely lie in the fine and detailed engravings which they contain, rather than in their descriptive passages which rarely exhibit any original observation or idea and are written in a dry and flat style as if the author were describing a list of items at an auction sale. John Britton's output must have constituted the coffee table books of their day, expensive and unwieldy as for the most part they were.

Of his native parish, Britton states in his autobiography that he would have written and published its history were the inhabitants 'sufficiently liberal and enlightened to encourage such a literary work'. I should have thought that even if they had been so they could not have afforded to purchase the same. John Britton was undoubtedly aiming at what we would call the top end of the market and I wonder if he cared much for the fate of his 'rude and illiterate village'. Yet perhaps he did, for in later life he sponsored a society in London to offer support to young men of his native Wiltshire who ventured to the capital to seek their fortunes.

His autobiography was published in 1850, when Britton was approaching 80 years. It was written, he explains, 'as a permanent Memorial to a large circle of kind friends, who, in the year 1845, volunteered as a Public Testimonial, in acknowledgement of the literary services they thought I had rendered to society'. There follows a list of the subscribers under the amounts subscribed — 5 guineas (the majority), 3 guineas, 2 guineas — totalling about £1,000. By this point in his life John Britton considered he had established himself as a respectable and respected figure of the literary establishment, no longer dogged by the privations of his early life.

His memoir begins as follows: 'On the 21st day of December, 1846, with the thermometer at 22°, and in the seventy-sixth year of my age, I commence writing a work which is intended to embrace a faithful and circumstantial memoir of my own public life and literary works.' It seems amazing that he should have recorded the temperature at the time of his putting pen to paper but John Britton was a faithful recorder of detail, of provided information, rather than an inspired descriptive writer, not to say coiner of original and sometimes fantastic ideas like his predecessor from Kington St. Michael, John Aubrey. Britton himself was undoubtedly very proud of his achievements. In the preface to his third volume of *Beauties of Wiltshire* he records that he had spent the previous twenty-five years 'actively and zealously devoted to the public service. . . . I have laboured hard, both bodily and mentally, to supply literary and historical gratification for lovers of topography and antiquity — and have executed, perhaps, more literary works, within twenty-five years, than any other English author.'

Apart from his books, John Britton's other legacy to his countrymen, particularly his fellow Wiltshiremen, was the foundation of the Wiltshire Archaeological and Natural History Society. Britton had written to Sir Richard Colt Hoare, the antiquary of Stourhead, around 1820, with the idea of forming a Wiltshire Topographical Museum and Library, offering his own collection if Hoare did the same. Hoare refused. He had helped Britton with information on Stourhead for volume 2 of his *Beauties of Wiltshire* and this volume was dedicated to Hoare. However, Hoare refused to co-operate with Britton on volume 3, which appeared much later, and Britton was distressed by what he described as 'jealous oppositon'. Hoare, for his part, declared himself to be uninterested in publications aimed at 'the tourist' rather than genuine antiquaries like himself. So in certain quarters at least, for all his ambition, poor John Britton was never quite accepted.

Much later, in 1852, at an advanced age, Britton presented his entire collection to the Wiltshire Archaeological and Natural History Society which was formed the following year. The first issue of the Society's *Wiltshire Magazine* gives a general account of that meeting and a transcript of John Britton's address, given in his 83rd year. He died on New Year's Day in 1857, aged 85.

6. MAUD HEATH'S CAUSEWAY AND THE MORAVIAN SETTLEMENT

Maud Heath's Causeway A well chronicled feature of the River Avon between Malmesbury and Chippenham is the causeway which is built beside the road from Wick Hill through East Tytherton, Kellaways and Langley Burrell to Chippenham. This route for pedestrians is named after one Maud Heath, a market woman and widow of Kellaways who, about 1474, gave to certain trustees some houses and land in and near Chippenham. The income from these was to finance the construction and maintenance of a causeway from Wick Hill to Chippenham. According to Canon Jackson, 'There can be no doubt that to ensure safe passage for the old wives and their baskets across this plashy level, was a main point with the considerate Maud Heath'.

So it is that for more than five centuries those travelling on foot have been able to go dryshod by this route. Today we only really notice the causeway where it is raised on arches to cross the Avon and its flood plain near Kellaways, but before the roadway was metalled the causeway, built of stone sets, would have stood out prominently above the mud and mire of the lane. The stone sets of Kellaways rock have now been metalled but the original paving may still be observed beside entrance gates to fields.

The monument to Maud Heath on Wick Hill was erected in 1838 at the expense of the Marquis of Lansdowne and William Bowles of Bremhill. This consists of a column on which sits a statue of Maud Heath with her basket and stick. At its base is inscribed the following verse by William Bowles:

> 'Thou who didst pause on this aerial hight
> Where Maud Heaths Pathway winds in
> shade or light
> Christian wayfarer in a world of strife,
> Be still and ponder the Path of Life.'

The causeway begins on the summit of the hill beside the road and progresses the 4½ miles to Chippenham, where its end is marked by an inscribed stone opposite St. Paul's Church:

Above: Wick Hill: Maud Heath's Monument

Below: Kellaways: Maud Heath's Causeway and Chapel

'Hither extendeth Maud Heath's gift
From where I stand is Chippenham Clift.'

Erected 1698 but given 1474

In 1698, too, a pillar was erected beside the River Avon where the causeway is raised on arches. This is inscribed to the memory of Maud Heath and has some Latin words transposed into English verse by William Bowles. This pillar has a sundial as does the monument in East Tytherton which was erected in 1974 to commemorate the half millennium since Maud Heath made her gift.

Moravian settlement   The first time I walked the length of Maud Heath's Causeway, from Chippenham to Wick Hill, I was surprised and intrigued by the impressive range of buildings, of which the Moravian Chapel is the centrepiece, which lie back from the road rather more than halfway along the causeway in the village of East Tytherton. I had never encountered a Moravian Church before, and the somewhat exotic-sounding name coupled with a long-standing interest in non-conformist sects encouraged me to find out more.

The Moravian Church had its origins over 500 years ago in Czechoslovakia, where a group of people, in protest at the moral corruption and political activity of the Roman Catholic Church in Bohemia, established a community apart where they lived in brotherly fellowship according to the principles of the Sermon on the Mount. They called themselves 'The Unity of the Brethren'. In 1467, with the creation of its own separate Ministry, this community withdrew from the Church of Rome and became the first independent Protestant church. Persecution did not prevent the new church from spreading throughout Bohemia and Moravia.

In 1620 Protestantism was overthrown in Bohemia and ceased to exist as an organised body. A few members secretly maintained its traditions in remote villages of Moravia and in 1722 some refugees settled on the estate of the Lutheran Count Zinzendorf in Saxony. Zinzendorf became their leader and was the coiner of the word 'ecumenical' and the ideas contained therein. In 1727, during Holy Communion, the congregation witnessed an outpouring of the Holy Spirit and all became convinced of their oneness in Christ. This dramatic experience strengthened the Moravians' belief in the unity of the Christian church and imbued them with a desire to carry the Gospel afar. After the renewal of 1727, missionaries went out to the West Indies, to South Africa, North America and England.

From 1736 the Moravian example attracted many Anglicans, including John and Charles Wesley, who for many years co-operated with the Moravians in the movement known as the Evangelical Revival. The Moravian Church grew slowly, however, since it saw its mission not so much to foster its own growth but rather to act as a leaven in the other churches.

In 1739 one John Cennick, a young man of Quaker background, came under the influence of Whitefield and Wesley in Kingswood, Bristol. He

John Cennick

separated from Wesley on issues of doctrine, but with Whitefield's authorisation he began an evangelistic campaign of his own in North Wiltshire. He was invited to preach at Castle Combe, then drew a large crowd at Langley Common, outside Chippenham. He toured the district, visiting Malmesbury, Somerford and Swindon, where he and his companions were fired upon, showered with mud and then with blood from local butchers, for the reason that Cennick preached so much about Christ's blood being shed for sin.

North Wiltshire had been an area strong in early nonconformity, especially Quakers, and many subsequently became followers of Cennick. The Societies which John Cennick established he regarded at first as offshoots of Whitefield's Tabernacle. His preachers formed themselves into a Wiltshire Association and in 1742 a centre was established at East Tytherton, a hamlet on the Avon meads without a church. Whitefield visited Cennick's Wiltshire Societies, but by this time Cennick was moving away from Whitefield towards the Moravian Brethren. With the approval of his followers, in 1745, John Cennick handed over his Wiltshire Societies to the care of the Moravian Church. Three years later he made a gift of the chapel and plot of land in East Tytherton. Much of his time from then until his death in 1755 was spent in long preaching tours of Ireland.

The German system of organisation was adopted and members were divided into 'choirs' or classes, according to sex and age. A Sisters' House was opened in 1750 for the reception and training of girls and single women who wished to improve their education or be employed in doing needlework, etc. This is on the right-hand side of the present chapel. On the other side is the Minister's house which, together with the chapel, was rebuilt later in the eighteenth century. Behind this range of brick buildings is a more imposing three-storey stone house — this is dated 1785 and was the School House. This was a ladies' school which took both boarders, among whom were many daughters of Moravian ministers and missionaries, as well as day girls from adjacent villages. Among the latter was Francis Kilvert's mother. The sisters' house closed in 1880 and the boarding school in 1940; it is now a private residence.

East Tytherton: Moravian Settlement

In his book, *History of Bremhill* (published in 1828), Rev. Bowles describes the Moravian settlement as 'an interesting Christian community' where 'industry, peace and the spirit of religion are predominant'. Bowles notes with satisfaction the good relations which existed between Moravians and Anglicans and that Moravians spoke of the Church of England 'with the greatest respect'. He also recalls with affection a former Moravian minister 'with whom the writer has lived in intimacy for the space of seventeen years'. Bowles says: 'The part of the parish which the united brethren inhabit has a peculiar air of comfort. The buildings consist of chapel, with a neat connected building for the minister, and another connected building appropriated to a young ladies' boarding school. These are educated without regard to particular creeds, but all morally and religiously . . . at a small distance a house for females employed in fine needlework . . . the young ladies of the school all similarly dressed in white, with a simple black ribbon'.

A service is held here each Sunday afternoon at 3.00 p.m. when a minister comes from Swindon. I attended a service here one Easter Sunday: on a crisp afternoon lit with brilliant sunshine I joined a handful of other worshippers in a simple, bright and flower-bedecked chapel. The strength of the singing compensated for the paucity of the congregation and the joyous praise filled the high-ceilinged old building.

Thus it was that East Tytherton became and remains to this day a Moravian centre. A Moravian church has survived in Malmesbury and Swindon, but all the other Societies which John Cennick founded hereabouts have been lost.

7. CHIPPENHAM TO BRADFORD-ON-AVON

Unlike Tetbury and Malmesbury, Chippenham expanded greatly in the nineteenth and present centuries, first with the arrival of the main-line railway in 1841 and subsequently with new industry. In common with other towns in North Wiltshire and Gloucestershire, Chippenham had, in addition to tanning, a significant wool and cloth industry. Chippenham was also an important route centre and was able to survive the demise of these traditional industries and indeed to prosper. The population has grown from 4,000 at the turn of the century to some 20,000 today, a scale of growth unequalled by any other Wiltshire town, except perhaps Swindon.

Before the railway, Chippenham had for many years been an important staging post on the London–Bath Road. The original settlement is sited on rising ground contained within a loop of the Avon, where it makes a sharp change from a north-westerly to a southerly direction. Modern building is concentrated to the north and west so that the old town centre has not been entirely submerged though much has disappeared in the course of redevelopment. The river swings north-westwards below Monkton Park and brings a refreshing breath of the upper Avon right into the town centre.

The Chippenham Town Trail, described in a leaflet published by the North Wiltshire District Council, takes advantage of this and consists of a circular walk including the riverside footpath through Monkton Park and the more interesting parts of the old town, including High Street, The Shambles, Market Place, St. Andrew's Church and, most attractive of all, St. Mary's Street. This last is a quiet backwater with buildings in a rich variety of styles overlooking the Avon. All are arranged along a street beneath the imposing walls of the town's main church. Chippenham Parish Church is a large building and exhibits many architectural periods from the Norman to the Gothic and even to the present century when the rood screen between nave and chancel was built.

The Yelde Hall in the market place is the oldest surviving building in Chippenham and probably dates from the late sixteenth century. The building originally served as town hall and court, and was subsequently an armoury for the local volunteers, a fire station, a lock-up and is now a museum. Chippenham Museum provides a striking contrast with the Athelstan Museum in Malmesbury. If Malmesbury has a restricted number

Chippenham: view from the Avon with the spire of St. Andrew's

of artefacts but is strong on explanation and presentation, then Chippenham is rather the reverse. It is a fascinating, sometimes bewildering, collection which demands time to be fully appreciated although one wonders how relevant are some of the exhibits. Down some steps in the old lock-up is an interesting collection of geological specimens which are well-labelled and mainly of local origin. I would have missed these altogether had I not asked the friendly curator whether there was a geological collection.

A glance at the Ordnance Survey map will confirm Chippenham's importance as a route centre. The London–Bath road enters via 'old' Chippenham and passes through the town from south-east to north-west. The main-line railway enters from the north-east via a cutting, crosses the London road by a viaduct and leaves the town to the south-west by an embankment. It seems a little odd that the two routes to and from the same points should cross each other here at right angles. A local branch line formerly left Chippenham to link Calne to the railway system and branches of the Wilts and Berks Canal once extended to both towns.

Writing in his book *Highways and Byways in Wiltshire*, published in 1917, Edward Hutton's opinion is that Lacock is 'easily the most remarkable and the most beautiful in all Wiltshire'. That view must be as convincing in the 1980s as it was seventy years ago. It is as though time itself had bypassed Lacock — with the exception of the village school (built 1824) and the Georgian façade of the Red Lion (1730s), the rest of the village consists of a fascinating mixture of buildings from the thirteenth to seventeenth

Lacock: view up East Street

Lacock Abbey: south front

centuries. There are styles of architecture and methods of construction from every period, and all manner of dwellings from basic cottages to grand houses. There is much worthy of note in the village including the Church of St. Cyriac, the tithe barn and the village cross, but this is not the place to describe it at all fully. A useful companion is, of course, Pevsner's volume on Wiltshire or, better still, the booklet *A Guide to Lacock*, which is available in the National Trust shop. Apart from most of the village, the National Trust owns Lacock Abbey and runs the Fox Talbot Museum of Photography.

The manor of Lacock was originally held by the Norman Earls of Salisbury and was inherited by Ela Countess of Salisbury who later married William Longespée, the son of Henry II and Fair Rosamund. Elsa was left a widow and, as a memorial to her husband, she founded the Augustinian abbey for nuns at Lacock. Six years later Ela took the veil and became the first Abbess. In 1257, at the age of seventy, she retired, and died in 1261 — her memorial stone can be seen today in the cloister. Three centuries later the Abbey was dissolved by order of Henry VIII. The property was soon sold to Sir William Sharington, who demolished the church and converted the convent into a manor house. Yet the new owner's alterations and additions have served to produce a manor house still recognisable as an abbey and a very beautiful building which really must be visitied. The ground floor is arranged around the cloisters, still quite intact, which lead to many rooms whose former functions are explained. The National Trust publish a booklet which describes the Abbey and its history more fully.

Lacock Abbey: east front from the Avon

Lacock Abbey came to the Talbots when Olivia Sharington married John Talbot of Worcestershire. John Aubrey recalls that 'Discoursing one night with her lover from the battlements of the abbey, said she, "I will leape downe to you." Her sweetheart answered that he would catch her then; but he did not believe she would have done it. Nevertheless, she leapt down and the wind, which was then high, came under here coates and did something to break her fall. Mr. Talbot caught her in his arms but she struck him dead; she cried for help and he was with great difficulty brought to life again. Her father thereon told her that since she had made such a leap she should e'en marrie him'.

A later member of the family is Fox Talbot, inventor of photography. The Photographic Museum, in a converted barn beside the main entrance to the Abbey, contains an interesting collection of early cameras and equipment, as well as some of the very earliest photographs ever made, by Fox Talbot, of details of the Abbey.

Melksham is a town about which few writers have much to say, and most of what is said tends to be negative. For example, in his book describing the architecture of the county, Nikolaus Pevsner says, 'Of all the small towns of Wiltshire Melksham has the least character and least enjoyable buildings'. Viewed from the south or west, one is confronted by industrial buildings and tall chimneys — nor is the High Street particularly attractive. The Avon flows through the town but with little effect — the main feature is a flood control barrier beside the rubber factory. The first time I ventured about the town on foot I was surprised, not so much by unexpected beauty, but simply by the unexpected. There is a large National Trust shop, a tyre museum, a shop selling Melksham Rock and a Japanese Restaurant, surely a rare combination of attractions!

There is a rich legacy of non-conformist places of worship here. Like other cloth-making towns, Melksham had a strong dissenting population. I was interested to discover that the present Spiritualist Church in King Street (next door to Quaker Cottage) was a Friends' Meeting House until 1950. This simple but elegant building dates from 1734, although Friends were well established here in the previous century. I peered over the wall at the rear of the chapel to discover the old burial ground — I saw one characteristic plain gravestone but could not make out whether this belonged to Rachel Fowler, a local Quaker of the last century. It was this good lady's habit to leave Bible tracts on her window sill for the edification of passers-by. Rachel Fowler did much charitable work in the town, including founding some almshouses; the modern Centre for Community and Arts is named after her. Perhaps Melksham's most famous son was one John Fowler who, in 1858, invented the steam plough, though I do not know if he was related to Rachel.

A spring was discovered at Bowerhill in 1815 whose waters were declared to possess medicinal properties. The three imposing pairs of houses known

Melksham Spa, c. 1816

as 'The Spa' which overlook the roundabout at Bowerhill were built as lodgings for the visitors who, unfortunately, never arrived. They look like a detached piece of Bath implanted here, between fields and a modern industrial estate. A walk down Church Street leads past 'The Round House' — formerly a drying house for cloth, and many older and more attractive houses towards Canon Square. To the left is the Church of St. Michael and All Angels, essentially a Perpendicular church, not especially interesting except perhaps for the stained-glass clerestory windows in which are depicted a number of Celtic and Saxon saints, including Aldhelm, and also King Alfred. Beyond the church is the tithe barn whose structure was severely altered in the last century by its conversion into a schoolroom.

With the exception of the incomparable village of Lacock and its Abbey, overlooking the river, this middle stretch of the Avon is the least rewarding part of its course from source to sea. It is possible to follow the river by footpath in a southerly direction and on through the grounds of the Lackham College of Agriculture towards Reybridge, but difficulties present themselves in attempting to extend this into a worthwhile circular walk. I have already described a six-mile circular walk based at Lacock in my previous book *Wiltshire Rambles*. This fine walk, although not strictly a 'riverside' walk, crosses the Avon at Reybridge and Lacock Bridge and, in between, proceeds by the towpath of the long defunct Wilts and Berks Canal, ascends Naish Hill to give splendid views north over the Avon Vale towards Chippenham, and continues by lane and through woods to descend by the grounds of Bowden Hill House. A much shorter walk, but one which follows the right of way along the riverside between Reybridge and Lacock Bridge is described here (Walk 8).

A field path exists between Lacock Bridge and Melksham east of the Avon — a distance of some three miles. This route is not especially attractive, however, and to return to Lacock on the west bank would entail walking along the busy Melksham–Chippenham road, which is certainly to be avoided. South of Melksham I have completed a circular walk starting at the Parish Church of St. Michael and All Angels, beside the former tithe barn and across fields to reach Boundary Farm and thence by a pleasant riverside footpath passing Monkton House on the opposite bank to reach the pack horse bridge at Whaddon. This neat stone bridge was constructed in 1725 to replace an earlier wooden structure. From here I followed fieldpaths to cross the railway and reach Broughton Gifford church, thence by fieldpath to emerge on a lane which leads to Broughton Common, a large expanse of land which was never enclosed. Past 'The Bell' pub and the Strict Baptist Chapel a track leads between houses to field paths and Norrington Common. More field paths take you to Melksham once more via an uninspiring complex of sewage farm, railway sidings and factories. This is a five- to six-mile walk and I could only recommend the first section from Melksham to Broughton Gifford: I have therefore omitted to include a detailed description of the route in the walks section of this book.

Further downstream no public right of way exists along the river between Staverton and Bradford-on-Avon, save for a short stretch south of the river which connects with the towpath of the Kennet and Avon Canal (Walk 9). This leaves the riverside footpath between Staverton and Whaddon and here it is possible to enjoy a good circular ramble of six miles — this route I have described in my *Wiltshire Rambles* so feel I cannot, in fairness to the reader, include it here too. In the absence of a detailed description, I offer a brief outline below.

From Holt Church descend by fieldpath towards the massive chimney which surmounts the Nestlé's factory at Staverton, cross the Avon and bear left just before the Methodist Chapel. The track becomes a footpath which leads you under the railway and thence by riverside path to Whaddon and its interesting little Norman church standing on a bluff above the confluence of the Semington Brook and the River Avon. From the church you continue to follow the riverside path to the pack-horse bridge, by field path to Broughton Gifford Church, and thence by bridleway through a succession of fields to the incomparable medieval manor house and chapel at Great Chalfield. From here the way is by well walked field paths back to Holt. This is a varied and rewarding walk and is easily followed with the aid of the relevant 1:50,000 scale map (or a copy of *Wiltshire Rambles!*).

Whaddon Bridge

8. BRADFORD-ON-AVON TO BATH

The common-place name 'Bradford' literally means broad ford. This feature, together with the existence of a hill rising steeply above the Avon, attracted early man to settle here. The indefinite remains of a prehistoric camp are situated on the hill top at Budbury. Roman artefacts have been found here which indicate that these later invaders recognised the advantage of this defensive position. A battle was fought at Bradford in 652 which secured a Saxon conquest over the British. Aldhelm, Bishop of Sherborne, founded a monastery here about 700 A.D. and this is the time from which the church of St. Laurence dates. The nearby Church of Holy Trinity dates from the twelfth century; when this much larger church was erected the tiny Church of St. Laurence became redundant and was eventually quite forgotten.

A nineteenth-century rector of Holy Trinity, Canon Jones, in preparing a history of his parish, describes his discovery of the old church as follows: 'In the year 1856, when standing at the highest point of our town close by St. Mary, Tory, my eye was attracted at what seemed to be the outline of an old ecclesiastical building, consisting of a nave, chancel and north porch. It was very hard to disentangle it from all the other buildings with which it was almost hopelessly intermixed.'* Canon Jones referred to William of Malmesbury's account of Aldhelm's founding of St. Laurence as corroborative evidence.

In 1872 the chancel was purchased from the owners, who used it as a gardener's cottage, and later the Charity School, till then located in the nave, was removed to the Church House. The modern house on the south side was demolished and the whole restored. The sculptured angels which had been placed over the porch of the modern house were later repositioned high above the altar. Accounts vary as to the date of St. Laurence but a major contemporary work† points out that 'recent careful inspection of the church has led to general acceptance of the belief that its main fabric is indeed the work of Aldhelm's period, early in the eighth century and that later details are of a restoration towards the end of the tenth century.' The church today seems small and simple with thick stone walls and narrow splayed windows. The building consists of chancel, nave and north porch; buttresses stand in place of a south porch. The dark interior is lit by narrow

*Jones, Canon W. H., *An Account of the Saxon Church of St. Laurence.*
†Taylor, H. M. & Jean, *Anglo-Saxon Architecture*, 2 vols., Cambridge University Press, 1965.

Bradford-on-Avon: Holy Trinity and the undiscovered Saxon Church, 1812

shafts of light — the nave is as high as it is long (25 feet) and the chancel (13 feet long by 10 feet high) is reached by a narrow, round-headed archway.

In 1001 King Ethelred granted the manor of Bradford to the Abbess of Shaftesbury and in the Abbey's hands it remained and grew in importance — King John visited the town in 1216. Holy Trinity was built in the twelfth century and the tithe barn in the fourteenth. In 1295 Bradford sent two members to Parliament. During these times the woollen trade was established. The first phase of this trade comprised the export of wool — by the thirteenth century wool had become England's major export and the basis of her wealth. The second phase began around 1300 and lasted until the mid-seventeenth century: most important now was the production of broadcloth which had been spun and woven locally but was exported to be dyed and finished on the Continent. In 1659 Paul Methuen, a leading local clothier, brought over spinners from Holland (who lived in that part of town known as Dutch Barton) and thereby developed the fine cloth trade. Following the collapse of the old broadcloth industry, with the application of new skills, the cloth was dyed and finished locally. A new era of prosperity dawned. This continued throughout the eighteenth century but began to decline in the following century. Then the centre of the industry moved to Yorkshire with its large mills, up-to-the-minute steam-driven machinery, willing workforce and forward-looking entrepreneurs. By 1850 the number of factories had been drastically reduced and the population of Bradford had begun to decline.

John Leland wrote of Bradford, about 1540, that 'all the toun standeth much by cloth making'. John Britton, in his *Beauties of Wiltshire*, published in 1801, writes as follows: 'The manufactories of Bradford are almost wholly confined to the clothing trade; it is the largest and most regular in the manufacture of any in Wilts, perhaps in the kingdom; one manufactory alone employs from one thousand to fifteen hundred persons.'

Britton's description of the town itself would be nearly as true today as it was in 1801: 'Bradford is built principally on the declivity of a hill; the houses are of stone. Many of them are exceedingly spacious and handsome, being erected and chiefly inhabited by wealthy clothiers. The streets are mostly narow and irregular. The surrounding eminences furnish some very pleasing views; and the prospect from the bridge is peculiarly romantic and picturesque.' The upright John Britton rails against Bradford's 'lower classes' for being 'immoral and unclean' and noted that they were, as a result, suffering from illnesses such as scrofula and even leprosy.

As the cloth trade declined, so, of course, did the fortunes of Bradford-on-Avon, along with those of many other towns in the West of England. This situation was eased somewhat with the advent of the rubber industry in the last half of the nineteenth century. Here were large empty mills and a ready supply of water. More than a century later the rubber industry is still happily flourishing in Bradford-on-Avon and helps to maintain, rather than destroy, the traditional character of a small industrial town in the country.

To describe Bradford-on-Avon is perhaps less easy for one who has lived here for three years than for one who lives elsewhere. After such a short time I feel so attached to the place that I am forever praising its virtues to people I meet. Before moving here my family and I lived in South Devon, between Dartmoor and the sea. My only reservation, if I have one, is that Bradford is not nearer the sea, but it is a comfort to know that the Avon is ever flowing towards it through this town. Before 1980 I had seen Bradford once, ten years earlier, when my wife and I caught a bus here from Bath where we were staying for a weekend. I remember crossing the bridge and looking up to take in that surprising view of the ranks of houses on the hillside. The tithe barn, too, did not fail to impress, with its massive proportions and atmosphere of cool peace (it was a hot day!). Three years after coming to live here it is still not possible to take the place for granted. Even the daily walk to my bookshop in The Shambles is a delight.

For most of these three years we lived at the top of Woolley Street so that the walk down towards the town took in the high stone wall marking the grounds of The Hall. The gables of this splendid early seventeenth-century house are clearly visible in winter but progressively less so as the tall trees (mostly horse chestnut) come into leaf. Woolley Street merges into Silver Street and I always enjoy the medley of pre-Classical gables and mullioned windows of some houses, the stately Georgian façades of others and the varied Victorian frontages of yet others. And those right-hand turnings uphill: Whitehill, Whiteheads Lane and Coppice Hill never fail to allure. It's good, too, to know that Bradford is not simply an 'olde worlde towne' with nothing to pride itself on but its delightful buildings and beautiful

Bradford-on-Avon: the 'Chapel' on the town bridge, 1894

situation — between Silver Street and the river stand the extensive works of the Avon Rubber Company making Bradford a significant centre of industry and employment.

In 1983 we moved to the west side of town and my route down is usually by Conigre Hill which is very steep where it descends via Tory, Middle Rank and Newton, then under the high medieval walls of the old Priory to reach Market Street. Once again the alternation of classical and pre-classical architectural styles is most evident. Perhaps the best example of this is on the far side of the Town Bridge where the tall windows and symmetrical façade of the Georgian Wine Lodge is sandwiched between the low gables, mullioned windows and steeply-pitched roofs of adjacent buildings. I suppose that, when the building which is now the Georgian Wine Lodge was erected it seemed like an act of vandalism to place this classical façade next to the old English vernacular buildings which abut it on each side. Yet how attractive and amusing and lively it all seems to the modern eye.

The architectural attractions of Bradford-on-Avon are many and diverse — the most well known include the fourteenth-century tithe barn, the town bridge (two arches of which are thirteenth century) with its 'chapel' (the present seventeenth-century building was used as a lock-up) and the Saxon stone Church of St. Laurence, opposite which is the later Church of Holy Trinity. A number of town trails are described in the Bradford-on-Avon Town Guide and walking around the town, including the hills, is the only

Bradford-on-Avon: the Avon in winter flood

70

way to truly appreciate the place. So many of the houses are on slopes that a different view is obtained from every spot and many of them are indeed surprising. One also cannot ignore the old industrial buildings — the former mills, once so busy in the processing of wool and the manufacture of cloth (many of these are seen on Walk 10). None has been so employed since the turn of the century. Abbey Mill was the last to be built, in 1875, and this is the tall and stately building visible downstream from the Town Bridge.

The course of the river from Bradford-on-Avon to Bath is, perhaps, the most beautiful stretch of all, and includes the famed Limpley Stoke valley. Considering the proximity of this district to the large town of Bath, it is remarkably unspoilt. Villages visible from the valley itself include Turleigh, Freshford, Limpley Stoke, Claverton and Bathford. All these places, with the possible exception of Bathford, have neither grown very much in modern times nor lost their individual character. There are more interesting villages close by in tributary valleys such as Iford and Monkton Combe, or on the plateau through which the Avon has cut, such as Westwood and Monkton Farleigh.

This is all good country for the rambler —there are many rights of way and, for the most part, they are not difficult to follow. The exception to this is the riverside path itself which exists only on the river's left bank from Avoncliff to Freshford Bridge, and a longer stretch from Dundas Aqueduct to Sheephouse Farm on the right bank below Warleigh Woods. I have included these riverside paths in circular walks described in my earlier book

Dundas Aqueduct

71

Where Wiltshire Meets Somerset, the first in the walk based on Avoncliff, via Freshford Bridge, Iford and Upper Westwood, and the second in the walk based on Dundas Aqueduct via Conkwell and Farleigh Wick. The Avoncliff walk is one of my favourites — indeed the right of way beside the Avon's major tributary, the River Frome, is outstanding all the way to Farleigh Castle. Once again I feel it would be unfair to the reader to include walks already described by me elsewhere, so it will suffice to include here a shortened version of the walk based on Dundas Aqueduct (Walk 11). In the absence of an unbroken riverside path between Bradford-on-Avon and Bath, an easy route which gives an unhindered view of the valley between these towns is provided by the towpath of the Kennet and Avon Canal which can be followed quite easily from the canal locks at Bradford to the pumping station just east of Bath and this is a route which should not be missed.

Though they cannot be described as riverside walks, the rights of way leading to Bathford Hill and Brown's Folly, to Bathampton Down and to Little Solsbury Hill all offer fine walking with spectacular views over the valleys of the Avon and By Brook and westwards to Bath.

Looking downstream from Dundas Aqueduct

9. BATH TO BRISTOL

Bath is, after London, one of the most visited and most celebrated cities of England. It has featured in so many books both of fact and fiction that a lengthy exposition of its history and architectural attractions, not to mention the many famous persons who have lived here at some time, seems inappropriate, although some brief account of Bath is certainly called for.

There are legends which tell the story of this spa town before the Roman invasion but it is the Roman baths which now form the visible ancient core of Bath. The Romans knew Bath as Aquae Sulis, the waters of Sul. One of the early discoveries of the Roman baths was made in 1790 when a stone depicting a male gorgon's head mounted upon the shield of Sul Minerva was unearthed. This was found to belong to a Roman temple dedicated to the patron goddess Sul Minerva, Sul being a local divinity and Minerva the Roman God of Wisdom. Discoveries continued to be made which led to the uncovering of a series of baths and swimming pools, sweatrooms which were heated by hot air passing under the floor (hypocausts) and cooling rooms. The Great Baths were discovered in 1890 and the Victorians restored the surroundings in the manner which they believed was extant in Roman times. Excavations continue until the present day and the story of Aquae Sulis is unfolding still.

The Romans left Aquae Sulis and Britain in the fourth century. The Saxons destroyed the city in 577 and the famous baths were abandoned and forgotten until their rediscovery in the eighteenth century. The Saxons later founded the Church of St. Peter on the present site of the Abbey and King Edgar was crowned here in 973. The importance of Bath as an ecclesiastical centre increased when the Norman Bishop, John de Villula, transferred his seat here from Wells in 1088. He built a large cathedral, only fragments of which survive in the present Abbey. This is almost entirely in the Perpendicular style, having been started in 1499 and left unfinished at the dissolution of the monasteries forty years later. The nave vault was built in the nineteenth century and replaced an earlier timber structure.

In common with other towns and villages along the Avon, Bath enjoyed a flourishing of the wool and cloth industry in these and following centuries; it was also noteworthy as a spa town. That indefatigable lady traveller, Celia Fiennes, visited the town about 1687 and found it still essentially a medieval town within its walls. She notes that 'the town and all its accommodations is adapted to the batheing and drinking of the waters'. Celia Fiennes describes in detail the baths and the manner in which visitors took the waters; the healing fluid itself, she says, is 'very hot and tastes like the water that boyles eggs'.

Taking the waters was primarily a medicinal exercise which could cure 'lameness and palsyes'. The only diversions were 'green walkes very pleasant and in many places' such as about the Abbey and King's Mead where 'there are severall little Cake-houses where you have fruit Sulibubs and sumer liquours to entertaine the Company that walke there'. Some forty years later, about 1724, Daniel Defoe visited Bath and writes that 'in former times this was a resort for cripples but now we may say it is a resort of the sound, rather than the sick; the bathing is made more a sport and diversion, than a physical prescription for health; and the town is taken up in raffling, gaming, visiting, and in a word, all sorts of gallantry and levity'. Defoe sounds regretful that Bath should have changed in this way.

Richard Nash, known as Beau Nash or the King of Bath, was appointed Master of Ceremonies in 1708 and remained so for the next fifty years. His aim was to reform Bath society. To this end he insisted on certain rules of behaviour; these were later formulated and posted in the Pump Room and included a ban on carrying swords and fighting duels, and enforced standards of elegance, taste and courtesy. His long-term objective was to transform Bath into a centre of fashionable society and a capital of English art and literature, and it must be said that in this he amply succeeded.

The rebuilding of the city now began, thanks largely to the enterprise of two men: Ralph Allen and John Wood. Ralph Allen began his career in a remote post office in Cornwall. He came to Bath as assistant postmaster at the age of 26 and devised a system of cross-country posts which obviated the need for all mail to first pass through London. This made him a fortune which he used to obtain the mineral rights over Bathampton Down and Combe Down. Here he opened quarries and mines to extract the local lime-stone ideally suited to building.

At the time Bath began rebuilding, a private company which included Ralph Allen as one of its treasurers acquired Bath Corporation's interest in the River Avon between Bath and Bristol, and after repeated attempts by the city fathers work now began on the construction of the Bath Navigation. In just three years from 1724 to 1727 six locks were built between the two cities and the Avon became navigable from Bath to the Bristol Channel. Railways were laid to link the quarries at Bathampton and Combe Down with the river so that blocks of stone could be more easily transported for building the new Bath and, indeed, traded down the Avon Navigation and beyond.

John Wood was an architect from Yorkshire who had a vision to build a city in the classical Roman style. When he was convinced that the Avon Navigation would be completed he began to think about improving the city and, in this, he was partly financed by Ralph Allen. His buildings include Queen's Square, the Circus and North and South Parades. Prior Park, Ralph Allen's great mansion in which he entertained his literary coterie, was built between 1734–41. John Wood the Elder died in 1754 and his son, John Wood the Younger, carried on as architect responsible for the Royal

Bath: Guildhall and Abbey, 1829

Crescent, the Assembly Rooms, and many of the new baths and streets of the city. Pulteney Bridge was built in 1770 by Sir William Pulteney to a design by Robert Adam, the Guildhall in 1775 and Lansdown Crescent around 1790. Urban development had ceased by about 1810–20 and the planned Georgian city which we see today is largely as it was completed at that time, although modern redevelopment and the Second World War blitz have taken their toll in the city centre.

In his work on Bath and Bristol, published in 1829, John Britton describes Bath, in his rather wooden style, as follows: 'Bath exhibits a series of handsome houses with free-stone fronts, covered by stone tiling, and ornamented with all the five orders, as well as many fancies, of architecture — whilst the streets are wide, the inhabitants gay, devoted to pleasure and amusements; and the surrounding scenery, though hilly and abrupt, is covered with fine turf, woods and varied plantations. The substratum is a bed of fine, soft, but durable free-stone.'

Bath is an incomparable city and its streets and open spaces must surely provide one of the most attractive and interesting townscapes in the country. The views along Georgian terraces are alluring, so too are the one hundred and one details of carved stonework, iron railing, or whatever. The city is also beautiful at a distance — I always enjoy the views from Bathampton Down and Bathford Hill. There, rising from the Avon valley to climb the slopes of Lansdown lies Bath, its terraces and crescents threading the hillside: ten thousand buildings of creamy stone reflecting the light set against the green hills all around. Under a sunny blue sky the contrast of colours is startling and the effect quite unforgettable.

The Avon Navigation between Bath and Bristol is still functioning and the towpath on the river bank provides a fascinating route well worth exploring. It begins at Pulteney Bridge and ends at the lock and weir at Hanham Mills where the Avon becomes tidal.

Approaching Pulteney Bridge from the east via Pulteney Street you can be quite unaware that you are in fact crossing the Avon. Look out for a gap just before the single storey shops which line the sides of the bridge — here are steps signposted 'To the Riverside Walk'. You descend to the left bank of the Avon, to the stepped weir and modern flood control barrier. The recreation ground is on your left and the Institution Gardens across the river on your right. You soon pass the lofty tower and spire of the Victorian St. John's Roman Catholic Church opposite and then walk beneath the main-line railway bridge. The rear of Bath Spa Station can be seen on the opposite bank. This was built in 1840 to a design by Brunel and carries the main line from Paddington to Bristol and beyond.

Bath: Pulteney Bridge and head of the Avon Navigation, 1829

The path now ascends past Widcombe locks on your left towards the road. The flight of locks here marks the junction of the Kennet and Avon Canal with the River Avon and has recently been restored. The engine house and chimney of a pumping station can be seen on the far side of the first lock — its function was to pump water back to the top of the flight. The railway down from the stone quarries on Combe Down met the river hereabouts, though nothing of the former workshops, wharves and cranes remains to be seen. One can imagine what a very busy point of the river this must once have been.

On reaching the road you bear right along the signposted 'Avon Walkway' to pass by the wrought-iron pedestrian girder bridge built in 1877 complete with tollhouse. This replaced an earlier bridge which collapsed into the river on the occasion of the Bath and West Show in that year, with the loss of nine or ten lives. You pass under the railway once again and cross the road bridge ahead to follow the towpath along the right bank. On the left bank is a series of tall factory buildings and, further along, the presnt works of Stothert and Pitt, an historic and important engineering firm, made famous worldwide by its cranes.

You pass under two road bridges, the second of which is a former railway bridge which once carried the Midland line from Mangotsfield and the Dorset and Somerset Branch Line to the terminus at Bath Green Park Station. The elegant mock Georgian façade of this building (built 1870) has been retained in the conversion of the platforms and trackbed into the approach to the new Sainsbury's Supermarket, the structure of which can be seen from the towpath. You can see Norfolk Crescent, built in 1810, through the hedge on the right and a little way before you pass under the pedestrian Victoria Bridge. This early suspension bridge dates from 1836 and its single span measures 150 feet.

Now the Avon curves gently to the left: the hill directly ahead is marked by the spire of the chapel in Locksbrook Cemetery, whilst the left bank is dominated by a series of gasometers. You pass under a number of bridges including Windsor Bridge and another crossing of the old Midland Railway to reach a fork in the river. This marks the first of the series of six locks on the Avon Navigation — the canal-like channel which the towpath follows on the right bank was cut when the Navigation was being built. The old stone humpback bridge ahead bears the date 1728; on the far side a notice issued by the Great Western Railway gives weight restrictions for vehicles crossing the bridge. The excavation of 'Weston Cut' created an island — this is known as Dutch Island on which once stood a brass mill belonging to a Dutchman named Nicholas Graef. The island is still used for industrial purposes but the only evidence of the old brass mill is the naming of Brassmill Lane which runs beside the towpath on the right.

You soon reach Weston lock and the end of the island. Looking back you can see the weir on the far side. The Lower Bristol Road, Twerton Wood and the main-line railway are visible on the left bank, whilst the towpath on the right bank proceeds past a number of modern factories and once again passes under a crossing of the old Midland railway. At last you feel you have left the city and reached the country. Straight ahead now is the singular-looking New Bridge or Weston Bridge or, as Pevsner has it, Newton Bridge. This is a stone bridge with a single 100-foot span and a series of flood arches on either side. An unusual feature are the roundels pierced straight through the spandrels of the arch. The towpath passes through the second arch on the right — just ahead are moorings beside a boatyard and the Riverside Café.

Cross the bridge, which formerly marked the boundary between the City of Bath and the County of Somerset, and descend to the river. The metalled path leads to a small works beside the river which is fenced off but to the right of which the towpath reaches a stile to follow the river bank. You follow the river bank for almost a mile until you pass under yet another former railway bridge. At the top of the hill and hanging woods on the far side you can see

Bath: New Bridge, 1830

the plain façade of Kelston Park, with its commanding view down to the Avon and southwards into Somerset. This house was built by John Wood the Younger, about 1770. It was the birthplace of Sir John Harington, godson of Queen Elizabeth I whom he entertained with such magnificence when she came to Bath in 1590 that he had to sell part of his estates to pay the bills.

You now approach the embankment of the main-line railway which follows the Avon and the towpath for about a mile to reach the lock and weir at Saltford. When the Avon Navigation was opened, coal was imported from Shropshire via the River Severn. The Kingswood colliers objected to this trade and in 1738 wrecked Saltford Lock in retaliation. As you approach the lock you must bear left to follow the boundary of a boat basin. Here the towpath passes between hedgebanks to reach the road. Turn right through the old part of the village. On the right are the remains of Saltford brass mill including an annealing tower — this was a furnace used to keep the alloy soft and workable. The road eventually reaches a T-junction with the 'Bird in Hand' pub on the right. Bear left here if you wish to visit the village church — this is found about 150 yards uphill by bearing right at the turning marked Queen's Square.

St. Mary's Church has a square tower, a plain structure save for some rather half-hearted pinnacles and battlements which surmount it. Apart from the tower, the church consists of a simple nave and chancel. A gallery in the nave and whitewashed walls lend it something of the atmosphere of a chapel, and very appealing it all is. There is a large and most interesting memorial stone in the porch under the tower, dedicated to one Frances Flood, an itinerant beggar woman from Devon who visited Saltford in 1723. the inscription reads as follows:

> Stop reader and wonder
> See as strange as ere was known
> My feet dropt off from my body
> In the midst of the bone
> I had no surgeon for my help
> But God's Almighty's aid
> On whom I always will rely
> And never be afraid
> Though here beneath intrd the ly
> Corruption for to see
> Yet they shall rise and reunite
> To all Eternity

Frances Flood was evidently a leper and, following her misfortune, wrote and had printed a tract whose words more or less corresponded to this inscription, the proceeds of which provided her with a living thereafter.

Another interesting memorial is to be found in the wall behind the lectern which is inscribed, 'Here lieth the body of Lamorock Flower who deceased the sixth day of April 1639'. Underneath is the following verse:

> Flowers the warshipt in ye springe
> Flourishing now with Christ their king

Flower was the name of the family which then lived in the manor house behind the church. This manor house is substantially Norman — the tall narrow windows and zigzag moulding decorating the window arch on the west front are unmistakable.

From the churchyard you can enjoy a wide view over the Avon valley. Due east is Kelston village and beyond it Kelston Round Hill, a conical hill crowned with trees; to its left is the flat-topped Lansdown where, in 1643, a fierce but indecisive battle was fought between the Roundheads and Cavaliers. The Cavaliers were led by Sir Bevil Grenville who had raised an army of 6,000 in Cornwall and was marching to join the King at Oxford. The Parliamentary General Waller was sent to intercept him and his army on Claverton Down, expecting his foe to approach from the south. The Cavaliers, unexpectedly, came along the Avon valley from the south. After a brief skirmish at Warleigh they reached Marshfield and Waller deployed his men and guns on the commanding heights of Lansdown between the Cornish army and the city. Grenville was killed in one of many charges on the Parliamentary forces. The Cavaliers fell back to Marshfield and next day marched to Chippenham and eventually beat Waller decisively at Roundway (i.e. 'Runaway') Down. The dissatisfied Roundheads meanwhile vented their frustration on Saltford Church, where they smashed all the stained-glass windows and removed the Norman font which was later rescued from use as a cattle trough.

From Saltford the towpath follows the left bank of the Avon, so, in order to complete the walk to Hanham Mills, you must cross the river here and walk along the road for half a mile in order to reach the right bank at Swineford. From the 'Bird in Hand' pub you descend towards the railway bridge and turn sharp right after passing under the bridge to follow an embowered track up to the railway which now forms a right of way for cyclists and pedestrians. Once across the river you leave the track and scramble down the side of the embankment to reach the river's right bank. Now follow the towpath to the next lock and weir and Kelston Mill, where a pair of annealing towers marks the site of a former brass mill dating from the late eighteenth century (Walk 12). From here you cross a couple of fields to reach the road and pavement. Walk through Swineford until you reach the 'Swan Inn'. Opposite here is a stile leading into a field. Follow the field boundary until you reach the riverside. The buildings on the left comprise Swineford Mill, a former copper works dating from 1840 but later converted to a flock mill.

The next two miles follow the towpath without event, save the confluence from the north of the tributary River Boyd and a final crossing of the abandoned Midland railway. Eventually you reach a large complex of industrial buildings — a former chemical works, dated 1881 — on the left bank. The river bends south towards Keynsham where the River Chew, a major tributary, flows north from the Mendips to meet the Avon. At the confluence of these rivers was sited a large brass works. The several brass mills on the Avon owe their existence to water power, to the raw materials zinc brought from the Mendips and copper from Cornwall. This industry prospered in the eighteenth century but declined in the following century in the face of competition from Wales — the last mill closed at Keynsham in 1927.

Downstream from Keynsham lock and weir the river swings to the north under the red-brick monster which comprises the Cadbury-Fry Chocolate Factory. Once past here you continue to follow the towpath along the right bank to cross the old humpback bridge over the tributary Warmley Brook beside some pleasant riverside meadows and hanging woods (Walk 13:1) to reach Hanham Mills and two neighbouring pubs, 'The Chequers Inn' and 'The Old Lock and Weir'. The latter indicates the position of Hanham Lock. The Avon Navigation ends here, after a series of six locks, and the tidal Avon begins. The next mile is through the hanging woods of Hanham Gorge and this extremely pleasant stretch is included in Walk 13.

An excursion from Bath down the Avon Navigation became a fashionable diversion after its opening in 1727 and regular services between the two cities were established by 1730. The journey took about four hours and cost one shilling. Princess Amelia went all the way to Bristol in a wherry when she was in Bath in 1728. For almost a century the barges were pulled by men rather than horses. A toll was charged on the weight of cargo or number of passengers carried and trouble often arose when barges failed to declare all they had aboard. The Avon Navigation was most certainly a great boost if not a necessary pre-condition to the rapid development of Bath in the eighteenth century.

10. BRISTOL TO THE SEA

The Port of Bristol's control extends up-river as far as Hanham lock and weir, so this seems an appropriate point at which to begin the last part of our walk down the Avon. The mile and a half by the towpath on the right bank through the wooded Hanham Gorge is a most enjoyable section and is included in Walk 13 from Hanham Mills. This gorge is not as spetacular as Avon Gorge on the west side of Bristol but has a similar origin. The river here cuts a valley to a depth of about 150 feet through a relatively hard rock — the Pennant Sandstone. This formation is of the Carboniferous Period and overlies the Coal Measures which outcrop further north in the Kingswood district where there was once considerable mining activity. The Pennant Sandstone is one of Bristol's favourite building stones and there is much evidence of quarrying in the sides of Hanham Gorge and further downstream, particularly on the east side of the loop which the Avon makes about Conham.

After following this loop the Avon heads north north-west below Troopers' Hill, and the towpath reaches the road which here follows the river very closely for a short distance. The road eventually diverges to the right and the towpath re-establishes itself beside the river. The wedge of low-lying land formed between the towpath and the road is now an expanse of flattened rubble partly enclosed by a stone wall — this was the site of a large copper works. Clues to its former use as such are given by the presence of dark copper slag blocks which are found interspersed with the mainly Pennant Sandstone walls and by the great chimney on the summit of Troopers' Hill which once constituted the outlet of a flue from the works. The smaller chimney to the right, below the hill, is also built partly of old slag blocks and marks the site of an old coal mine — the Coal Measures are here interbedded with sandstone and outcrop on the flank of the hill.

Further downstream the river curves west and then south-west — the extensive site of the former St. Anne's Board Mills, now sadly closed and in the process of demolition, stretches along the south bank for almost half a mile. The towpath eventually emerges at the head of the Feeder Canal which gives craft access from the Avon to the Floating Harbour and takes water from the river to top up the harbour. The Feeder Canal was cut in the first decade of the 1800s as part of the Floating Harbour project to improve dock facilities in Bristol. As you cross the bridge over the Canal you can see the lock at its head and down the Avon itself to a V-shaped weir. Bear right after crossing the canal to follow the road by the left bank towards the Floating Harbour.

The 'island' formed by the Feeder Canal to the north and the course of the Avon to the south is known as St. Philip's Marsh and is almost a wholly industrial area, as is the north bank of the canal. As you approach the road bridge at the point just before which the Feeder Canal enters the Floating Harbour you bear right via Avon Street. This is very much an industrial area too — there are some modern buildings but many stone-built Victorian edifices and railway lines crossing the street. One of the most striking buildings is a high rectangular brick factory with towers at the corners bearing the sign 'Gardiner of Bristol' — this is a former soap works built a century ago and now converted to other uses. As you pass beneath the main-line railway you can see the pinnacles of Brunel's magnificent Temple Meads station buildings on the far side of the river. At the end of Avon Street you must cross the multi-lane Inner Circuit Road, then bear right and left by Narrow Plain and right by Queen Street. The Courage Brewery is on the far side of the Avon. The way beside the river is through Castle Park below the bombed-out shell of St. Peter's Church. This leads you down to Bristol Bridge which is sited on the original crossing point of the River Avon.

There is no evidence of Bristol's existence in Roman times; Brycgstow appears in the Anglo-Saxon Chronicle in 1063 and Bristou in the Domesday Book. The name means 'the site of the bridge', and this early bridge across the Avon, the proximity of a headland which stood clear of the surrounding marshy ground and the fact that this elevated site was almost entirely surrounded by water, led to the development of the original settlement. At that time the tributary River Frome encircled the higher ground to the north, west and south and joined the Avon just below Bristol Bridge. A moat was dug to link the Avon and Frome and the waters enclosed about thirty acres which contained the walled city and Bristol Castle. Much of the Castle was subsequently destroyed by Cromwell and today practically nothing remains.

The Anglo-Saxon Chronicle's account of Bristol mentions that the city enjoyed a sea trade with Ireland. This later extended to other parts of the Viking Empire such as Iceland and Denmark. After the Norman Conquest trade prospered with the establishment of the wine trade with France and the Iberian Peninsula. In 1240 the River Frome was diverted from the southern flank of the castle to a course due south to meet the Avon. A new quay was built here known as St. Augustine's Quay, the land having been bought from St. Augustine's Abbey.

By the fourteenth century Bristol had become the most important port of the West of England. Exports included wool, cloth, tin, and lead whilst wine, spices, oil and tar were imported. In 1373 Bristol was granted county status and its boundaries extended to include the seven miles of the Avon to the sea and the Bristol Channel as far as Steep Holm. A rich and powerful merchant class developed whose appetite for new markets led them to sponsor voyages across the Atlantic in search of new lands. In 1480, twelve

Bristol Bridge

years before Christopher Columbus, there was a failed attempt to discover America from Bristol, but in 1497 John Cabot, a native of Venice, left Bristol with a crew of eighteen in *The Matthew*, a ship of 50 tons. They succeeded in reaching the North American mainland. Bristol thereafter played a major role in the colonisation of the New World and the opening up of trade with those colonies. This in turn led to the development of new industries such as tobacco processing, clay pipe making and sugar refining — the first sugar refinery in England was established at Bristol in 1612. Prisoners and indentured servants were sent out to man the plantations in the West Indies and North America, but demand soon outstripped supply. Slaves from West Africa made up the shortfall; the heyday of the slave trade was from 1660 to 1786, when the campaign to abolish the trade began.

By 1700 Bristol was second only to London in size and importance as a port, its prosperity resting on the trade with West Africa and the New World. Glass making was an industry which mushroomed at this time — glass bottles were in great demand for bottling imported wine and water from the Hotwells and this latter commodity was exported in quantity. Chocolate manufacture was another local industry which grew with the importation of cocoa from West Africa. Privateering and piracy also contributed to the growing prosperity of Bristol throughout the eighteenth century.

At the beginning of that century Bristol still had a medieval appearance, walled and gated as it was. The city is graphically described by Celia Fiennes when she visited it in 1698, as follows: 'Bristol lyes in a bottom the greatest part of the town, tho' one end of it you have a pretty rise of ground; there are 19 Parish Churches beside the Cathedrall which has nothing fine or curious in it; the buildings of the town are pretty high most of timber work, the streetes are narrow and something darkish, because the roomes on the upper storys are more jutting out, soe contracts the streete and the light; the suburbs are better buildings and more spacious streetes. . . . This town is a very great tradeing citty as most in England, and is esteemed the largest next London; the river Aven, that is flowed up by the sea into the Severn and soe up the Aven to the town, beares shipps and barges up to the key, where I saw the harbour was full of shipps carrying coales and all sorts of commodityes to other parts; the Bridge is built over with houses just as London Bridge is, but it's not so big or long, there are 4 large arches here; they have little boates which are called Wherryes such as we use on the Thames, soe they use them here to convey persons from place to place; and in many places there are signes to many houses that are not Publick houses just as it is in London; the streetes are well pitch'd and preserved by their useing sleds to carry all things about.'

As at Bath, extensive building and rebuilding in the eighteenth century transformed the city and greatly expanded it: new neighbourhoods were planned including squares, crescents and parades of terraced houses, particularly to the north and west of the city, including the fashionable resort of Hotwells. The city centre was largely rebuilt too; John Wood the Elder was employed to build the Corn Exchange in 1742. If the age of discovery had been Bristol's first golden age, then the eighteenth century was its second. Yet by now the port facilities were becoming outdated and inadequate: Bristol was a tidal harbour which proved inconvenient as well as hazardous to the ships using it. Docks were constructed at Sea Mills in 1712 and at Hotwells in 1765. The City Council was concerned to extend and improve the harbour by this time, but it was not until 1809 that the Floating Harbour scheme was completed.

Bristol: Floating Harbour and view towards Bristol from Welsh Back, 1830

This rendered some two-and-a-half miles of the River Avon into a wet dock and created 85 acres of dock space. Lock gates were erected at the end of Cumberland Basin to connect the dock with the river. The river was channelled via the New Cut, direct access to which was gained via lock gates in Bathurst Basin. The Feeder Canal was also constructed to give access to the Avon Navigation to Bath and opened up a new industrial area around St. Philip's Marsh. The Floating Harbour allowed ships to enter the docks at high tide and then float unhindered to be unloaded and loaded. The cost of building was much greater than estimated and the Bristol Dock Company raised dues accordingly. This had the effect of reducing traffic and much trade was lost to other ports, notably Liverpool. Eventually the Dock Company sold the docks back to the City Council in 1848 and they reduced charges. This brought a temporary respite from decline. It soon became clear, however, that the navigation down the Avon between Bristol and the sea was impossible for the increasingly large cargo-carrying ships which were being employed. Traditional industries, such as sugar refining and glass, disappeared and the long and inevitable decline of Bristol Docks set in. The day was saved by the construction of entirely new docks, designed for much larger ships, first at Avonmouth in 1877, then at Portishead in 1879. Most recently the Royal Portbury Dock on the opposite bank of the river to Avonmouth was opened in 1977. The Floating Harbour's use as a commercial dock virtually came to an end in the late 1960s and it is now being developed as a waterway for recreational purposes.

Bristol has played an important part in the history of England. Although it did not grow as fast as most cities during the industrial revolution of the nineteenth century, it had been foremost in the discovery and colonisation of the New World which helped lay the foundation for the later prosperity of the whole nation. The city has witnessed many stirring scenes, particularly during the Reformation, Counter Reformation and Civil War. Following the Royalist defeat at Dunbar, Charles II crossed the Avon by the Hotwells to Rownham ferry disguised as a serving woman and made his escape to France.

No account of Bristol is complete without mention of the great engineer, Isambard Kingdom Brunel. His contributions included the Great Western Railway, Temple Meads Station, essential improvements to the Floating Harbour to prevent it silting up, and S.S. *Great Britain*, the world's first iron-hulled, screw-driven ship, which is now being painstakingly restored in dry dock at Bristol. Most impressive of all Brunel's Bristol masterpieces is, to my mind, the Clifton Suspension Bridge. Work was begun on this magnificent structure in 1831, but, owing to lack of funds, was not completed until more than thirty years later, after Brunel's death.

Before we continue our walk along the Avon from where we left off at Bristol Bridge, I feel I must record the fact that after walking by many hundreds of people fishing along the banks of the Avon, I actually saw someone land a fish for the first and only time at Bristol Bridge. It was a tench, about the size of a banana. This fisherman told me that the usual catch was dace or roach but that he had that morning caught a two-pound bream. From Bristol Bridge I followed part of the walk described in the booklet entitled *Bristol City Docks: Maritime Walks*, published by Bristol District Council.

From Bristol Bridge you follow the right bank of the Floating Harbour via Welsh Back, so-called because the ships formerly using this part of the docks were mainly engaged in the trade with South Wales. A glimpse along the picturesque and fascinating King Street on the right reveals the ancient pub known as the 'Llandoger Trow', a Welsh-sounding name indeed. I am quite sure a book could be written on this one Bristol street; I intend here to keep to the river bank as nearly as possible. Another building which cannot be ignored is the former Victorian warehouse, now music club, known as 'The Granary'. This is a splendid example of the ornate and colourful brickwork known as Bristol Byzantine which flourished among the city's industrial buildings at this time, other examples of which can be seen in the course of our walk through the Floating Harbour. On this far side of Welsh Back are two large and derelict warehouses — the second and later one bears the letters W.C.A. — the Western Counties Agricultural Cooperative Association.

86

Bristol: the Granary

Now cross Redcliffe Bridge, a drawbridge no longer used as such, and follow the pavement on the right beside the roundabout and under the magnificent Church of St. Mary Redcliffe, which, especially from this vantage point, appears larger and more impressive than Bristol Cathedral itself. St. Mary Redcliffe is, however, a mere parish church, largely built in the fourteenth century from the proceeds of the booming woollen trade and thanks, in particular, to the beneficence of the wealthy Bristol merchant, William Canynges. The initiative for its restoration in the nineteenth century came from John Britton, the Wiltshire antiquary, as early as 1842. On the corner opposite this wonderful church is an infinitely less grand, but not insignificant contribution to the welfare of present Bristolians by their forebears. This is the little garden, a former Quaker Burial Ground dedicated as such in 1666 and given to the city by Bristol Friends as a haven of peace and refreshment in the present century.

Take the first right by the 'Merchant Venturer' pub along Redcliffe Parade, a row of handsome Georgian houses. Just opposite the end of the brick-faced terrace is the top of a former donkey ramp leading down to the quayside. Near the bottom on the left is a gated entrance to Redcliffe caves. The official guide suggests that the sand from these man-made caves was used first as ship's ballast and later as the raw material in the local glass industry. The worked-out passages were then used for storage and waste disposal. The sandstone here is red (hence Redcliffe) and friable. It is identified as the Butcombe Sandstone of the Triassic Period. In the absence of a bridge across the entrance to the Bathurst Basin you must follow the quayside beside the 'Ostrich' pub and Bristol General Hospital. There is a former exit from the basin into the New Cut in the far corner.

Bristol: Floating Harbour and view towards St. Mary Redcliffe, 1830

Continue below Bathurst Parade and some attractive former warehouses to reach the main body of the Floating Harbour once again. You cross Prince Road swing bridge to reach Prince's Wharf, with Bristol Industrial Museum on your left. Opposite is St. Augustine's Harbour, into the head of which flows the culverted River Frome and now entirely restored or redeveloped. On Canon's Marsh to its left stand three large tobacco bonded warehouses and, behind, the towers of Bristol Cathedral and University. Prince's Wharf leads on to Wapping Wharf and then you must forsake the quayside to pass by the dry dock which holds Brunel's famous iron ship, S.S. *Great Britain*. You reach the water again at Albion Dockyard, now full of private craft, and proceed along Baltic Wharf.

On the far side of the Floating Harbour is Hotwells Dock and one of the last commercial uses of Bristol City Docks, viz. the delivery of sand for the local building trade. The three vessels *Sand Sapphire*, *Sand Diamond* and *Harry Brown* seem enormous compared to the assorted ferries, cruisers, sailing boats and sailboards but help maintain something of the atmosphere of what the city docks must once have possessed. One can further sense that atmos-

Above: Bristol: Avon Gorge and Clifton, 1830

Below: Bristol: Suspension Bridge at Clifton, c. 1890

phere from the sheer scale of the Floating Harbour, from the evidence of presrved warehouses, cranes, railways and all the other necessary dockside paraphenalia and also from that long list of evocative-sounding names such as Nova Scotia Place and Baltic Wharf.

From this last we must go by road via Albion Place opposite another three massive tobacco bonded warehouses, then by Cumberland Basin to reach the farthest westerly point of the 'island' formed by the Floating Harbour and the New Cut. Between this point and the Harbour is a fascinating system of locks and bridges which range from Brunel's swing bridge of 1840 to the new Plimsoll swing bridge of 1965. The aspect from the western tip downriver to Clifton Suspension Bridge and the Avon Gorge is quite stunning, giving contrasting views according to the state of the tide. Bristol City Docks and the journey down the Avon Gorge to the open sea was a prospect which must have impressed itself deeply upon young sailors making their first voyage, as well as upon the many thousands of hopeful emigrants who left their homeland by this route, many of whom had probably never before seen the sea.

The towpath along Avon Gorge is well worth walking and is included in Walk 14. The valley below Clifton Suspension Bridge is about 300 feet deep with its sides very steep if not vertical. An eighteenth-century traveller, Rev. S. Shaw, in 1788 describes an excursion from Bristol to Hotwells and to 'those tremendous rocks, which seem rent asunder by some extraordinary violence of nature'. He later describes the view from Clifton Down where he saw 'The tide-swoln river roll thro' the stupendous cliffs beneath, whilst the objects on and about its waves appeared in perfect miniature. We saw too the shuddering sight of men working out limestone from amidst the perpendicular sides, every moment in imminent danger'.

Further downstream, in the vicinity of Sea Mills, the land on either side of the river subsides. Sea Mills is on the site of the Roman port of Abona which was reached by road from Bath. From here men and supplies were shipped to the frontier region of South Wales. The Avon is deflected via the Horseshoe Bend to the south-west by the resistant Old Red Sandstone formation below Shirehampton Park; the folded strata can be seen outcropping on the river bank below the railway line. This section of the river was the most difficult for the larger ships to navigate and the section between Horseshoe Bend and Pill is known as the Hung Road where vessels would rest and wait for the tide and for river pilots from nearby Pill. Beyond Pill the Avon flows beneath the graceful arch of the new motorway bridge and then widens between Avonmouth Docks on the right bank and the more recent Royal Portbury Dock on the left, access to both of which is from the Bristol Channel rather than the River Avon.

From its humble beginnings amid the foothills of the Cotswolds in Gloucestershire, the Bristol Avon flows through the north-west quadrant of Wiltshire. From Wiltshire it enters the new county of Avon where once it marked the boundary between Gloucestershire and Somerset. The once great port of Bristol, of course, owes its existence to the Avon and the moorings it provided, with man's help, until ships grew too large to negotiate the river from Avonmouth. Now the commercial traffic has all but deserted the city docks in favour of the much larger facilities near the river's mouth.

Perhaps at the end of our walk down the Bristol Avon we are permitted to strike a philosophical note and I should like to quote a piece from the book *The Bristol Avon* written by one Ernest Walls and published in Bristol in 1927: 'The birth, the life and death of a river seems so strangely like our own. It is filled with the inevitable, yet slightest circumstances influence it. It ends by merging its individuality in that which is of like stuff yet which is immeasurably greater. It is always renewing itself, its life is ever being re-created'.

Avonmouth: the Avon meets the sea

'The stream invites us to follow: the impulse is so common that it might be set down as an instinct; and certainly there is no more fascinating pastime than to keep company with a river from its source to the sea.'

W. H. Hudson
Afoot in England

THE WALKS

Christian Malford: All Saints

A Note on the Walks

The walks described here are each accompanied by an appropriate sketch map to show the route taken and the main features encountered. The maps together with the detailed description should be sufficient to guide the rambler, but the relevant Ordnance Survey maps are always very useful companions. The countryside is constantly changing: ways become overgrown, field boundaries appear and disappear, features such as stiles and gates are subject to rebuilding or resiting — in such cases consulting the O.S. map will usually overcome uncertainty. Only two 1:50,000 'Landranger' maps are needed, as follows:

Sheet 173: Swindon and Devizes
Sheet 172: Bristol and Bath

All public rights of way on these maps are shown in red.

The more detailed 1:25,000 maps which include the Bristol Avon within their scope are as follows:

Sheet ST 98: Malmesbury
Sheet ST 97: Chippenham
Sheet ST 86/97: Melksham
Sheet ST 66/76: Bath and Keynsham
Sheet ST 67: Bristol (East)
Sheet ST 57: Bristol (West)

The Melksham and Bath and Keynsham maps are the 'Pathfinder' second series which show public rights of way in green whilst the earlier first series do not. The first series should therefore be used in conjunction with the 1:50,000 sheets.

Key to maps:

Lane or Road		Woods	
Track		Railway	
Footpath		Canal	
River or Stream (arrows show direction of flow)		Buildings	

1 TETBURY

via Long Newton, Fossey Way, Shipton Moyne and Estcourt Park

Distance: 6½ miles

With extension to Brokenborough 8 miles

GOING This is an easy and pleasant walk which includes a mile along the Tetbury–Malmesbury road in addition to riverside paths, field paths, drives and a section of the Roman Fosse Way. The extension to Brokenborough is a little more difficult and this can be avoided. There is the 'Rose and Crown' pub at Brokenborough and the 'Cat and Custard Pot Inn' at Shipton Moyne, besides many good spots for a picnic, in particular the bridge which carries the Fosse Way across the Avon.

From the old Market House in the centre of Tetbury walk through the Market Place and turn right into Silver Street, then follow the road out of town as it bears left down Fox Hill. This is the Malmesbury Road and crosses the main branch of the Tetbury Avon via Wiltshire Bridge, or Long Bridge as it is also known.

The old coach road leaves our route by a narrow track which serves the houses to the left of Wiltshire Bridge and reaches a footbridge. The Wiltshire Bridge is so-called because the boundary between the counties of Gloucestershire and Wiltshire was formerly defined by the Tetbury Avon. Carved into the north parapet of the bridge directly over the stream are the letters G/W, i.e. Gloucestershire and Wiltshire.

Follow the Malmesbury road for a little over a mile. This is a high road with a pavement and offers unobstructed views in all directions: particularly striking is the view back towards Tetbury with the tall, slender spire of St. Mary's Church rising from the jumble of rooftops. You reach a pair of lodges on either side of the driveway to Estcourt House (a former Georgian mansion now demolished), opposite which there is a milestone. Pretty soon the church tower of Long Newnton comes into view across fields to the left; the church tower itself is Perpendicular though all else was rebuilt in the last century.

As you reach a cluster of buildings around the road junction ahead you must cross the road to follow the pavement on the left-hand side. After a slight dip the road begins to rise again. Look out for steps leading to a

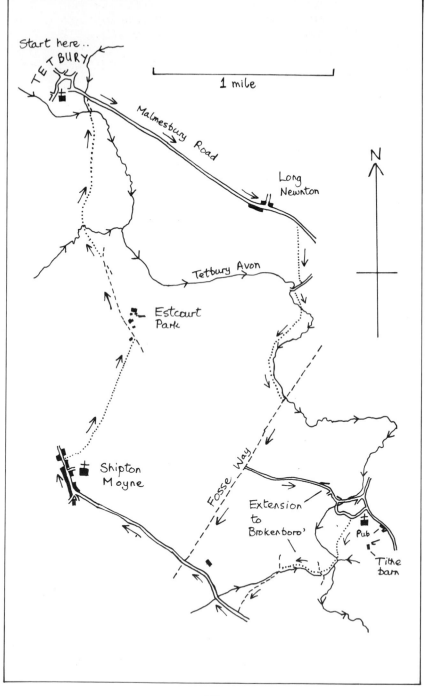

Start here..
TETBURY

Malmesbury Road

1 mile

Long
Newnton

N

Tetbury Avon

Estcourt
Park

Fosse Way

Shipton
Moyne

Extension
to
Brokenboro'

Pub

Tithe
Barn

massive stone stile on the left. Just opposite is a wooden stile in the iron fence which gives access to a field on the right. Cross this stile and head diagonally across the field towards a clump of trees. Pass the trees on the left and continue in the same direction towards a gate in the woods ahead. Go through the gate and follow the sunken path down to the lane below, where you turn right to reach the river.

As you turn into the lane you can see rocks exposed in the cutting on the right. This is Forest Marble, which is composed of thin slabs of shelly limestone (the main walling and roofing stone in these parts) interspersed with clay. It is not a true marble but is capable of taking a polish.

Just before the bridge you go through the gate on the left and follow the river downstream. Pass through the gate at the end of this field, cross the bridge on the right, then pass through a second gate. Now follow the track ahead as it climbs the terrace above the river. Follow the edge of the plateau to the right of the wooded slope towards a gate in the stone wall. Bear slightly to the left towards a gap in the wooded slope; once you have entered the wood by the gap the path becomes clear.

You leave the wood by a gate to enter a field — now go straight ahead by a path which wends its way along the river bank to a gate and stile; continue to follow the footpath to leave the field by a gate which drops you down into a sunken way: this is the Roman Fosse Way which marks the present boundary between Gloucestershire and Wiltshire.

To your left is the Tetbury Avon crossed here by an old stone bridge. Our route, however, leaves the river at this point and follows the Fosse Way in a south-westerly direction, i.e. turn right as you leave the field. The shorter route follows the Fosse Way until it reaches the minor road where you turn right to reach Shipton Moyne. As you approach Shipton Moyne you can see the tower of the village church and to the right across fields the twin domes of Hodges Barn, formerly dovecotes possibly of the sixteenth century, converted into a house before the Second World War. The church is reached by a driveway from the village main street.

You pass the unusually named 'Cat and Custard Pot Inn' on the left. Once past the pub on the right-hand side beyond the house named 'Simonswald' is the entrance to a walled footpath. Follow this right-of-way and cross the stone stile at the end to enter a field. Head diagonally and to the left across this field to a gate near the top left corner. From here bear right to follow the track the few yards to a gate on the left. Pass through here to enter a field which you cross diagonally to reach the stone wall opposite. Follow the stone wall until you reach a stone stile which you cross to enter another field. Now cross the field to reach the gabled house ahead. Leave the field by a gate and bear left to follow the drive through Estcourt Park.

As you leave the trees to cross a cattle grid the drive forks: take the right fork and head directly towards the spire of Tetbury Church. At a point where the drive is joined by another from the right, cross the wire fence into the field on the left. Now cross the field in the same direction you have been taking. Keep the wood on the left and begin to descend to a tributary stream of the Tetbury Avon. To the left of the fencing there is a little wooden footbridge across the stream. From here bear right over a stone stile, then left and right to reach a gate and stile to enter the field above.

From here you bear left and follow the field boundary to reach a stile, then a track which crosses your path. Climb the stone stile opposite and follow the stone wall on the right to cross a second stile, then a third. The valley of the Avon can now be seen sloping away to the right. As you begin to descend, make for a gate slightly to the left to leave the field and cross the river. Here you can see two sources of the Tetbury Avon uniting just upstream from the footbridge. Now follow the track until you reach Malmesbury Road, where you bear left to cross Wiltshire Bridge, then climb Fox Hill to reach Tetbury.

1.1   Alternative extension to Brokenborough: 1½ miles

Brokenborough has an ancient church, tithe barn and pub. The route from Brokenborough to the road for Shipton Moyne partly follows the Avon and a tributary stream and is a pleasant riverside walk.

Follow the Fosse Way south westwards from the point where you joined it as it climbs out of the valley formed by the Avon to reach the plateau. At a point where the green track becomes roughly metalled there is a turning to the left towards Brokenborough. Turn down here. Before you begin to descend look ahead beyond the turret of Brokenborough Church towards the half-ruined hulk of Malmesbury Abbey and the stranded tower of St. Paul's to the right. These are about two miles distant.

As the lane descends towards the Avon you pass Brook Farm, then bear right at the road past a disused chapel, then right towards the Church of St. John the Baptist, consisting of nave, north aisle, chancel, porch and bell turret. From the church the village pub, the 'Rose and Crown', can be reached by retracing your steps to the road and turning right towards Malmesbury. A hundred yards or so past the pub can be seen a medieval tithe barn, still part of a working farm. Its appearance from the road is not unlike the great tithe barn at Bradford-on-Avon, though not in such a good state of preservation. The steeply-pitched roof has, unfortunately, been stripped of its stone tiles and covered with corrugated iron. A lean-to has been erected between the two porches — these two porches do not have counterparts on the west side; they do not form 'transepts' as they do in Bradford-on-Avon.

To continue the walk: follow the lane below the church in a westerly direction to leave the village. When the lane bears to the right you bear left to enter a field by a gate. Head straight across this field. To the left is the tithe barn, its west wall blank except for a number of buttresses. When you reach the hedgebank ahead do not go through the gate at the corner which projects into the field but bear left and follow the hedge until you reach a wooden stile. Cross into the next field here and descend to a footbridge below at a point where the Avon swings to the right. This is not the large steel structure with gates on each bank but rather the bridge formed by a steel girder and handrail.

Now follow the riverside footpath, then a wire fence on the left until you reach a tributary stream which you follow upstream to a gate. Go through here and through a second gate which is a few yards further along on the left. Now follow the tributary by a path which is screened from adjoining fields by poplars and pine trees. You emerge from this riverside path onto a track which you follow until you reach a lane. Bear right here and follow the minor road some 1½ miles in a north-westerly direction to Shipton Moyne.

After passing Fosse Farm on the right you cross the Fosse Way and the boundary back from Wiltshire into Gloucestershire. Shipton Moyne is less than a mile ahead and the route from there back to Tetbury is given above.

2 SHERSTON

via Pinkney, Easton Grey and Fosse Way

Distance: 6 miles

GOING   The Sherston Avon has a character of its own and this easy walk
is a varied and enjoyable one which meets the river at several points
including the delightful village of Easton Grey. The return includes a long
stretch of the Fosse Way, here an embowered track hidden away from the
open country through which it slices. There are pubs and shops in Sherston
and 'The Eagle' at Pinkney.

From Sherston church you take the road opposite — Noble Street, which
leads out of the village in a southerly direction. As you descend you will see
some steps on the right which are reminiscent of The Chipping in Tetbury
and lead up to houses and an old Primitive Methodist chapel. On the left is
another flight of steps which leads up the bank at the side of the road to an
estate of new houses. You climb these steps and follow the path across the
cul-de-sac to continue by the path opposite to reach a stone stile. Cross here
and follow the right of way by the left-hand side of the field. Cross a wooden
stile at the end of this field and cross the succeeding field towards another
wooden stile; then leave this field by a stone stile to reach the lane.

   Turn right here and follow the lane down to a bridge across the Sherston
Avon. Now bear left by the lane signposted to Foxley and Malmesbury.
Follow the lane uphill until you reach the edge of the wood on the left. Turn
left along the track signposted to 'Keeper's Cottage'; there is also a public
footpath sign indicating the right of way to Pinkney. Follow the track ahead
until you pass through an iron gate to reach a crosstrack. Bear left here
towards the farm buildings at Pinkney. If you continue past the farm, cross
the river and climb up to the Sherston–Malmesbury road you will find 'The
Eagle' pub on the right.

   To continue the walk look out for a public footpath indicating the right of
way to Easton Grey through the farmyard towards a gate opposite. Go
through here to enter a paddock. Leave by a gate in the top right corner,
then bear left to reach a field by a stile. Now follow the left-hand boundary of
this large field: the river is visible below on your left. The soil in this field is
littered with pieces of flaggy limestone — this indicates an outcrop of Forest
Marble on this ridge.

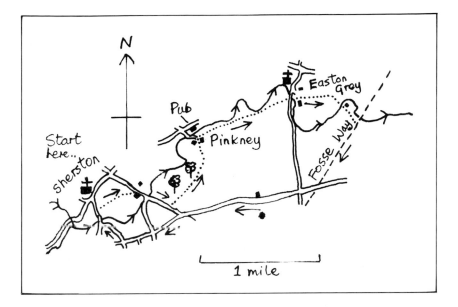

When you reach the far side of this field cross a stile and continue to follow the river. Soon the river takes a sharp turn to the left, but the right of way continues in the same direction across the projecting spur to resume its familiar course above the river on the far side. As you cross the spur here you can see the grounds of Easton Grey on the opposite bank and the elegant eighteenth-century pile of Easton Grey House on the hill.

Cross a stone stile and then a barbed-wire fence to reach the next field; now follow the fence on the left. The hamlet of Easton Grey now comes into view and you should forsake the fence and head across the field towards the centre of this cluster of buildings. You will soon find the ancient bridge as you descend to the river. Cross this five-arched bridge and turn sharp right past the old stone houses on the far side. Follow the lane up to the entrance gates of a big house and bear left by the edge of a field (there is a bungalow on your left). Cross the stile ahead to enter a field. Follow the field boundary on the left and cross the fence ahead to enter the next field. The right of way crosses this field to the bottom right-hand boundary, but respect for growing crops would suggest following the right-hand boundary to reach the same point. Leave this field and descend by the right-hand boundary of the next. When the hedgebank swings to the left you should leave this field by the narrow track which leads directly down to the river and a derelict mill — you can hear the rush of the water over the weir before you see the building.

This old mill makes an interesting study. The river is deep and still above the weir. The weir itself and the sluice gates which controlled the flow of water to the mill are still pretty well intact. The mill stream has been filled in but you can clearly see the direct course which it formerly took to the mill. Inside the mill you can find exactly where the mill wheel was situated. You can also see a couple of old grinding stones, each between about four and five feet diameter. They are made of a sandstone conglomerate rock which is very hard and therefore better suited to the grinding process than the local limestone. At the back of the mill you can see the course of the tail race as it follows a narrow channel to join the river further downstream.

From the mill you follow the track up and away from the river. This way soon rejoins the river — follow the track until you descend to a three-arched stone bridge across the river. This bridge marks a crossing point of the Fosse Way, here a mere cart track on either side of the river. This is also the halfway point of the walk. From here you bear right to follow the Fosse Way for a little over half a mile until you reach the lane. The Fosse Way here is a fairly wide track between hedgebanks. It crosses a wide ridge, for the most part, and so is dry going. You can see the church tower at Foxley across the fields to the left.

When you emerge from the Fosse Way bear right and follow the lane to the crossroads. Go straight over at the crossroads to follow the lane signposted to Sherston. This lane is not much frequented by traffic and, anyway, has a wide grass verge on either side for pedestrians. Now simply follow the signposts back to Sherston until you reach the River Avon and Noble Street.

3 MALMESBURY

via Great Somerford, Little Somerford and Lea

Distance: 8 miles

GOING   This walk is mainly by field path; it is not very well signposted but the way is made easier by landmarks visible along each stage of the walk. There are pubs in all three villages. You may be tempted to include a visit to Dauntsey which can be reached by a quiet lane from Great Somerford — this is about a mile each way.

From the main car park at Cross Hayes in the centre of Malmesbury make for Silver Street in the south-east corner. Silver Street leads to Back Hill, a sort of miniature version of Chipping Steps in Tetbury, by which you reach St. John's Street. To the left you can see Goose Bridge over the Tetbury Avon and this you will cross at the end of the walk as you re-enter the town. Now you turn right past the Court House and the Almshouses to reach the main road. Here you turn left to cross the Sherston Avon, keeping to the pavement on the right-hand side. By doing so you can avoid the roundabout which carries the bypass east of Malmesbury.

Walk down the Chippenham Road, past Burton Hill School on the right and Malmesbury Hospital by the pavement on the left. A short distance after passing Threshing Barn Cottage and just before the pavement ends look out for a gap in the wall on the left. Climb up here and then cross the wooden stile to enter a field. Head diagonally across this field aiming for a point just to the left of the buildings ahead: to do so you should reach a gap in the hedge on the far side. You leave this field by a gate just to the left of the farm buildings. Cross the track here and enter the next field; ahead of you stands an impressive group of buildings — this is Cole Park.

Head across the field towards a point a little to the right of the big house. As you get closer you will see a wooden stile beside a fence. Cross the stile and follow the fence in front of Cole Park House.

From here you can get a good view of the eighteenth-century façade of Cole Park Houuose — you will have seen less grand and older buildings behind as you approached the moated site.

Continue in the same direction by following the field boundary on the left. As you crest the gentle rise ahead you should look back for a last view towards Malmesbury. Descend to enter the next field and continue to follow

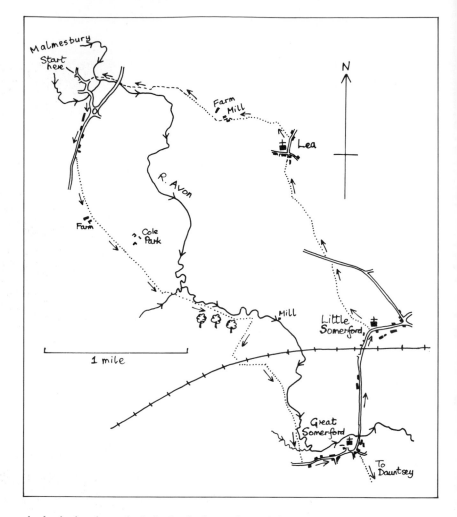

the hedgebank on the left. At the boundary of this field you enter the next by crossing an old wooden gate and a low barbed-wire fence beside the hedge. Now head diagonally across the field and to the left. The hedgerow opposite grows on the banks of a tributary stream of the Avon known as Gauze Brook. Follow the stream until you reach a footbridge. Once across you follow the riverside meadow in the same general direction.

This is the most rewarding part of the walk. The meadows are flanked by Angrove Wood on the right and the River Avon on the left; on the opposite bank the flat meadow rises a hundred feet or so to Maunditts Park Farm — this is the site of the former Manor of Little Somerford.

The first riverside field ends at a point where Angrove Wood almost touches the river. Here you cross a stile to reach the next field. Cross a second stile and follow the wood on the right. Eventually the wood ends —

104

bear right here across a wooden footbridge and on towards a gate. Follow the hedge on the left until you reach a further gate. Go through here and bear left towards the tunnel under the railway. On the far side of the embankment you bear left towards a gap in the hedgerow and then a little to the right to reach a further gap. Head straight on towards a gate in the far corner of the field where the hedge meets the river.

Follow the riverside footpath with Great Somerford and its church drawing closer downstream. Eventually a footbridge crosses a stream which runs into the Avon; from this point head straight on up the field ahead. The very pronounced ridge and furrow sculpting of this field is surely evidence of the strip field method of cultivation of medieval times. One often sees this in fields near village centres which were once arable but are now kept for grazing. On the far side of the field you reach a stile and the road where you turn left towards the village. Follow the road past the church and through the village to cross the Avon and head north to Little Somerford. If you wish to extend your walk to Dauntsey with its manor house and St. James Church with its amazing doom painting, then you should bear right down Park Lane and take the signposted public footpath on the right across fields to reach the lane which bears left towards Dauntsey.

From Little Somerford church you have a choice: you can continue along 'The Street' towards the main road and bear left by the 'Little Somerford Arms' pub or, if you do not wish to visit the pub, you can reach the next stage of the walk by field paths from the church.

To follow field paths bear right on leaving the church and right just past the half-timbered house through a steel gate to enter a field. Follow the field boundary on the left and head towards a gate in the far boundary. Go through this gate and follow the field boundary on the right to a gap at the top. Follow the hedgerow to the left-hand corner where you go through a gate and cross the field directly to reach another gate and the road. Bear left to follow the road for a short distance.

The routes now converge: when you reach a drive on the left cross the road and enter the field opposite by a wooden gate, somewhat dilapidated. From here you can see the church tower at Lea — this is the next objective. The right of way crosses the field diagonally to the bottom left corner but the sight of an arable field might encourage you to follow the field boundary on the left. Enter the next field by a gap in the hedge and follow the left-hand boundary until you reach a gap in the hedge and a wooden stile by which you enter the adjacent field on the left: follow the field boundary on the right to reach the iron gate, not on the right, but at the top of the field. Go through here and bear right through the iron gate just beyond on the right to follow the hedgebank on the right, then straight on to the bottom left-hand corner of the field where you cross a stile to reach the field on the left, then leave this field a few yards further on by a stile in the bottom right-hand corner to reach an enclosed footpath which leads directly to a squeezebelly stile and the road below Lea Church.

Take the road straight ahead, past the 'Rose and Crown' pub and before the old Zion Chapel look out for a stile on the left to enter a field. Cross the field diagonally and to the right. From here you can see the tower of St. Paul's Church in Malmesbury. Enter the next field by a gate and descend by the hedgebank on the left. At the bottom you meet a tributary stream of the Avon and head across the next field towards a gate to reach Crabb Mill (dated 1832). Now follow the metalled drive to cross the stream. Look out for a stile in the fence on the left which you cross to climb the slope in order to reach a second stile — now turn left and follow the hedge on the left until you cross a stile and reach a gate by which you enter a fenced track. This reaches the metalled drive serving the waterworks and this in turn leads you through the embankment of the former Malmesbury branch railway, then beside the Avon and under the new road bridge beyond which you continue in the same direction by the street known as Baskerville. You cross the Avon by Goose Bridge, then bear right by Back Hill to reach Silver Street and Cross Hayes Car Park.

4 CHRISTIAN MALFORD

via Avon Weir and Sutton Benger

Distance: 4 miles

GOING   An easy walk across the level Avon meads between two villages which face each other on opposite banks of the river. There is a choice of three pubs in Sutton Benger.

From All Saints Church in Christian Malford make for the stile in the churchyard wall opposite the porch and head across this large, open and very gently sloping field to follow the river in a southerly direction until you reach the far boundary. The crossing point is about 200 yards to the left of the river bank: here are a pair of stiles either side of a footbridge across a ditch. In the next field you continue in the same direction and make for a point just to the right of a group of farm buildings which can be seen just below the railway embankment approaching from the left. Go through the gate in the far left corner and follow the hedgebank on the left to reach a further gate.

Turn right to follow the grassy track towards the river. Cross the river by the modern flood control unit to reach the track on the opposite bank. Now follow this track as it bears right and then left to reach the road. Cross the road and follow the track directly opposite. When you emerge into a field follow the left-hand field boundary to reach a gap in the far left corner. Head diagonally across this field to the top left corner and pass through a gap to enter the next field. Now bear right and walk across the field towards a projecting hedgerow — the corner of the next large field is marked by a tree stump.

Cross into this field and follow the edge of the field with the hedgerow on your left — Sutton Benger and its church tower is clearly visible ahead. You leave this field by a gap in the hedgerow to cross the remaining field to reach the modern housing estate. Bear left at the top of Neville Terrace in order to meet the main road through the village.

From All Saints Church take the lane which leaves the village main street. Bear right at the 'Vintage' public house — there is a signpost indicating a public footpath to Christian Malford Bridge — and cross the stile in the corner at the end of the car park. Head diagonally across this field towards a stile by which you reach a track. Follow this track between hedgebanks until

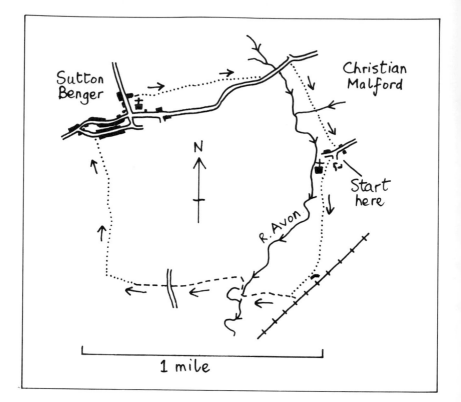

1 mile

you enter an open field. Follow the hedge and then cross the field to a point a
little to the right of the brick-built gun emplacement on the far side. Cross
the fence into the next field and follow the line of telegraph poles to reach a
gate in the bottom right-hand corner. The road on the right is raised above
the low-lying fields on either side by a series of arches through which the
river flows in time of flood. Leave the field by the gate and bear left to cross
the Avon.

A tributary stream can be seen joining the Avon just upstream from the
bridge: this is the stream that flows from Kington St. Michael through the
grounds of Draycot Houose. Immediately past the bridge turn right by the
indicated public footpath to Christian Malford Church. The right of way
actually crosses the field towards a hedgebank on the left. Follow the hedge
to reach a crossing point into the next field — this is a pair of stiles either side
of a footbridge across a ditch. Now follow the track which rises gradually and
takes you to a stile to the left of the council houses which encompass the
church on the north side.

5 SUTTON BENGER

via Draycot Church, Draycot Cerne, Kington St. Michael and Kington Langley

Distance: 7 miles

GOING   This is a varied and interesting walk with exceptionally good signposting. Nevertheless, some of the footpaths and tracks are not so easy: the sunken tracks beyond Draycot Cerne can be heavy going after rain and, beyond them, the embankment of the A429 must be negotiated to reach Kington St. Michael. There is a pub — the 'Jolly Huntsman' in Kington St. Michael and no less than three pubs in Sutton Benger. A shorter alternative walk of 4½ miles from Sutton Benger via Draycot Cerne and Kington Langley but omitting Kington St. Michael is outlined at the end.

Leave Sutton Benger by the main street and head towards Chippenham in a westerly direction. There is a pavement all the way up and over the gentle hill and down to the lodge house — a distance of about ¾ mile from Sutton Benger church. Bear right at the lodge house and walk down the drive beside a row of stately Douglas Firs. Cross the bridge over the stream which has here been widened to form the central feature of Draycot Park. The little Early English Church of St. James, with its many beautiful lancet windows, is charmingly situated on rising ground on the far bank.

From Draycot Church retrace your steps across the bridge and bear right to head upstream. Here you head through a narrow strip of woodland between the stream and the adjoining field. It is not very far to reach the road. Cross the road and bear slightly to the left to reach a gate and stile by which you enter a field on the far side. Cross the slope to reach a gap in the hedgerow — now you can see the hamlet of Draycot Cerne ahead. Note also the diminutive chapel to the left. Cross the next field towards another gap, then the last field to reach the lane just below the Grey House.

Turn left and, on the right, look out for a public footpath sign past the houses on the right, indicating Day's Lane: 1 mile. Enter the field here and head down to the bottom left-hand corner where you go through a gate and follow the hedgebank on the left through a long, narrow field to reach a stile. You now have a choice of ways though neither is particularly easy. The most direct way is to go straight on by the sunken track. After rain this track flows with water and demands wellington boots. The alternative is to bear right by

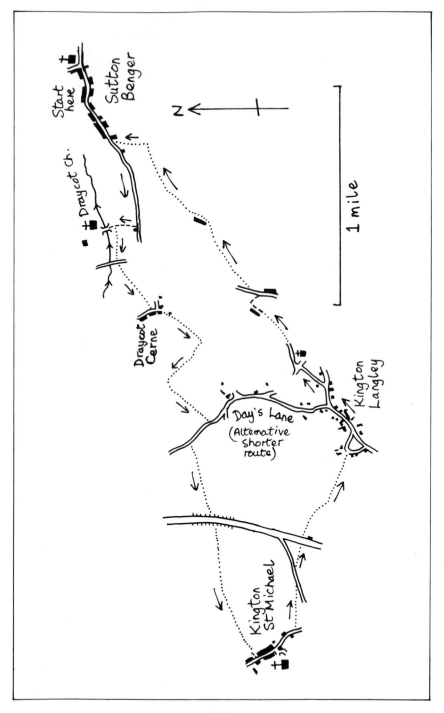

Start here

Sutton Benger

† Draycot Ch.

Draycot Cerne

Day's Lane
(Alternative shorter route)

Kington Langley

Kington St Michael

N

1 mile

110

the bridleway between hedgebanks. This way, too, can be wet but improves as it rises out of the valley bottom. This bridleway is narrow and tends to be pretty overgrown in summer but your efforts will be rewarded when the path bears left after reaching the top of the hill when there are some long views to the west and north.

Whichever way you choose you will eventually reach Day's Lane where you bear right to reach the next stage of the walk. This begins where the lane descends to reach the Draycot stream. On the far side is a public footpath sign indicating a way to Kington St. Michael through the fields on the left. Enter the field here and follow the riverbank towards the road embankment. There is no right of way under the embankment so there is no alternative but to climb the slope, cross the dual carriageway and descend the slope on the far side.

From the top of the slope you get a good view towards Kington St. Michael and the large field you must cross to reach it. Having descended the slope you cross the fence and the footbridge, then find a gap in the hedge beyond to enter the field. You must cross this field to a point in the far boundary; if there are growing crops or the field has just been ploughed you may be deterred — the right of way actually plunges straight through this field but if you follow the right-hand field boundary you will find the exit about 100 yards to the left of the top right corner. Here you go through a gap in the fence and follow the straight track beside the hedge directly towards the village. Bear left on reaching the village street and head past Lyte's Almshouses, the 'Jolly Huntsman' pub and St. Michael's Church to leave the village.

As you climb up Tor Hill to reach the last houses at the southern end of Kington St. Michael you enter the field on the left by a gate. Head diagonally across this field to reach a gate on the lane. Cross the lane to reach a gate opposite and a little further on. Head diagonally across this field to a point a little to the left of the row of white-painted houses facing the main road ahead. To the left of the horse trough is a gate leading to the road. Cross the road and walk up the drive to Courtfields until you reach a gate on the right. Go through here and head diagonally across this field to reach a gate in the far left corner where you follow the field boundary on the left to reach a gate: now follow the track ahead as it rises beside the hedgebank on the right. At the top of this track go through a gate. The signpost here indicates the footpath back to Kington St. Michael as 'Old Coffin Way' — this is presumably the direct pedestrian route to Kington St. Michael along which the Langley dead were carried to be buried at St. Michael's Church.

You emerge onto The Common at Kington Langley and bear left. You pass the United Chapel and the school by the wide green at the centre of the village and carry on towards the little nineteenth-century church of St. Peter. Here you take the left fork along Church Lane to Day's Lane and 'The Hit and Miss' pub. Cross Day's Lane and proceed by Silver Street, past the Primitive Methodist Chapel and on to the lane's end beside a house. Head straight on in the same direction to cross three small fields by three

111

stiles until you emerge onto a track serving a few houses on the left. This track bears right to reach the road.

Turn left here and look out for the next stage of the walk marked by a public footpath sign indicating Sutton Benger to the right. Enter the field and follow the left-hand edges of a number of fields ahead. Proceed to the right of the farm buildings; enter a field to the right of the last building (a bungalow) and head straight across the field to reach the next field through the hedgerow opposite. Now follow the hedge on the left: in the last field bear left to reach the road just to the left of the farm buildings. At the road turn right to reach Sutton Benger.

5.1   This is a shorter alternative to the above via Draycot Cerne and Kington Langley but omitting Kington St. Michael.

Distance 4½ miles

GOING   This alternative route is shorter and avoids the embankment of the A429 and the large open field between that main road and Kington St. Michael.

When you have reached Day's Lane from Draycot Cerne turn left rather than right, and take the right fork in order to reach the open green and the centre of the village. Then bear left to reach St. Peter's Church and Church Lane where the route back to Sutton Benger can be followed as described above.

6 CHIPPENHAM

via Monkton Park, Kellaways and West Tytherton

Distance: Distance 6 miles

GOING   This is a pleasant and varied walk by an assortment of riverside paths, field paths, farm tracks and lanes, and includes the raised section of Maud Heath's Causeway at Kellaways. There are no pubs on the route of this ramble although the 'Brewery Arms' in Langley Burrell can be reached by a short detour on Maud Heath directly from Kellaways. There are some excellent spots to enjoy a picnic, particularly beside the Avon. It should be noted that the field paths between Monkton House and the old railway bridge across the Avon and from there northwards along the river to meet the path from Cocklebury are not designated rights of way but rather permissive paths — the route is certainly well used and has been for many years, but this is by courtesy of the landowners.

Leave the Emery Lane Car Park in Chippenham by the approach road from St. Mary's Street and bear left. St. Mary's Street is probably the most attractive street in Chippenham and contains a diversity of houses from the sixteenth to the nineteenth centuries. Notice how low are the entrances to the houses on the left of the road whose surface has been progressively built up over the centuries: many of the houses are entered only by descending two or three steps. The former National Schools and Church of St. Andrew are on the right. Just past the churchyard look out for a cut on the left which carries a footpath down towars the River Avon. Here you cross the river by a footbridge: now follow the metalled path up the bank towards a point to the left of Monkton House.

At the rear of Monkton House bear right. Once past Seymour House you leave the metalled path and make your way by a worn path across rough land by the boundary of the golf course. Follow this way as it bears to the left; on the left are the back gardens of houses in Villiers Close while to the right is a wide sweep of open land held in a loop of the Avon — this constitutes the former grounds of Monkton House. When you reach a gate on the right you go through it to enter the field — now strike a course across the field and rather to the left. This takes you past a solitary beech tree on your left and on to reach a stile and footbridge across a brook. Now you follow the riverside path below Riverside Drive. At a point where the river

113

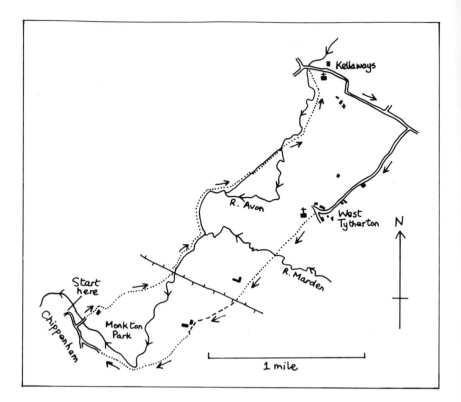

makes a curve towards the houses you must climb up to the road and descend the far side. Eventually you reach a stile below the redundant piers which carried the Calne Branch Railway across the Avon. Cross the stile and follow the riverside path. You pass a number of stiles and the confluence of the River Marden on the opposite bank.

About half a mile from the old railway bridge you cross a stile to enter a wood — follow the footpath through the wooded riverbank to emerge into a field. Continue in the same direction by following the hedgerow on the right. Now bear left to follow the hedge and ditch on your right. You leave this field by crossing the hedgerow by a plank bridge across a ditch to enter the next field. Now bear right across the main ditch and then left to follow the hedgebank and ditch on your left. You can see the buildings of West Tytherton away to your right.

At the end of this field you reach a bridge across the Avon. Before you cross the river notice the rock outcropping in the river bank. This is the Kellaways Rock, a locally-formed limestone which occurs here in the Oxford Clay. This limestone contains many fossils and some good specimens can be found on the edges of the fields hereabouts. Cross the river and bear left to follow the riverside footpath all the way to the raised section of Maud Heath's Causeway at Kellaways. The approach to the road gives a good view across the field to the causeway raised on arches.

At the road turn right to follow the causeway past Kellaways Chapel. Carry on until you reach a turning on the right signposted to West Tytherton. Follow this lane past some attractive old farmhouses: Curricomb, Gaston's and Bosmere Farms, until you reach Manor Farm — the large and rather grand stone house on the right. The windows to the left of the doorway are wide and mullioned and seem to be of the seventeenth century whilst those to the right are tall and closely spaced cross windows suggesting a later date. The road takes a sharp left here — you should cross the road and head through a pair of squeezebelly stiles to reach the entrance to the churchyard. St. Nicholas Church consists of nave, chancel and bellcote, is largely of the Early English Period and worth seeing. The first object you notice is the impressively proportioned Norman font, then the fine arcade joining aisle and nave.

From the churchyard entrance bear right across the field towards a gate south of the church. Enter the next field: the right of way heads straight through the middle of this field but you may be persuaded to follow the hedgerow on the left. Either way takes you to a footbridge across the River Marden. On the opposite bank you continue in the same direction to make for a point just to the left of the bungalow on the hill top ahead. Leave this field by a gate and then head straight on to follow the metalled drive. You cross the course of the old Calne Branch Railway and head on and down towards a group of farm buildings.

Once past the farm you enter the field on your right by the wooden stile. Cross the field to the far corner and enter the next field. Now follow the hedgebank on your right until you approach a white-painted building which you pass by crossing the stile to the left. Follow the worn path below the fence to reach the Avon. Now follow the riverside path to approach Chippenham. At the end of the open grass field bear left to reach the exit of the field in the top left corner. This takes you up to Badon's Lane, The Butts and then St. Mary's Street, St. Andrew's Church and the entrance to the Emery Lane Car Park.

7   EAST TYTHERTON

via Wick Hill, Bremhill and Stanley

Distance: 5 miles

GOING   This is an exhilarating walk which begins and ends in the quiet and pleasant village of East Tytherton. Maud Heath's Causeway ascends the Corallian escarpment at Wick Hill and affords views across the Avon meads and in the other direction towards the Marlborough Downs. Bremhill is an attractive village with an old cross and curiously-named pub 'Dumb Post Inn'. The lane downhill looks across the verdant Marden valley towards the thickly-wooded hills of Bowood. The last leg of the ramble crosses flat meadows at the foot of the escarpment.

From the square facing the Moravian Chapel in East Tytherton you take Maud Heath's Causeway beside the road signposted to Bremhill. Follow the road as it crosses the course of the old Wilts and Berks Canal, which follows the foot of the escarpment here, and begin to gain height, first by the scattered houses and farms of Bremhill Wick and then more directly as the road swings to the left to ascend Wick Hill. The climb rewards you with some splendid views over the Avon meads towards Chippenham and Derry Hill.

Just at the point where the road levels out Maud Heath's Causeway terminates. The stile on the left leads to the column supporting Maud Heath's statue while the stile to the right leads to a ridge top path. Our route follows the road straight ahead to reach the T-junction. Cross the road and climb the stile into the field. The public footpath sign indicates Bremhill straight ahead. As you cross the field here you will see the church tower and roof tops of the village and down towards Calne and beyond towards the chalk downs of Roundway Hill above Devizes. You may notice the reddish, sandy soil hereabouts — the underlying rock here is the Corallian, which is limestone interbedded with sandstone. The subsoil is quite porous and the ground here is always easy going even after rain.

Head straight across the field towards the stile opposite. Cross here and follow the hedgebank on the right until you reach a stile. Cross here and bear left down towards the footbridge across a ditch. Now climb up to the right-hand side of the house above to reach the road. Bear left into the village. Notice the terrace of houses on the left and the attractive warm tint of the

116

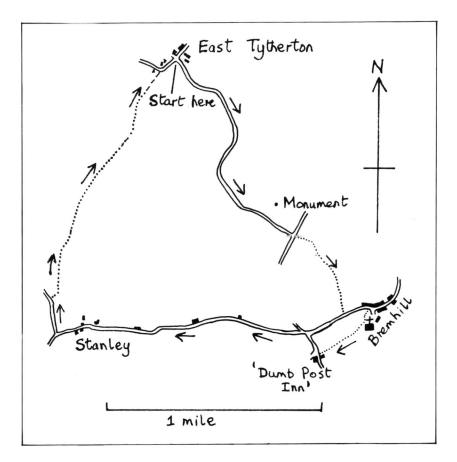

East Tytherton

Start here

N

Monument

Bremhill

Stanley

'Dumb Post Inn'

1 mile

stone of which they are built. This is locally quarried Corallian limestone. The key to the church may be obtained from the shop in the village centre. St. Martin's Church is not especially attractive, heavily restored as it was in the last century, nor is there much evidence of its former rector, Rev. William Bowles. The back of the rectory and something of Bowles' Gothic ornamentation can be seen from the churchyard.

To continue the walk: leave the churchyard by the gate directly beneath the tower. The right of way bears a little to the left to pass by the left of the house ahead. Now follow the ridge top path with the hedgebank on your right and the valley of the river Marden and its tributaries below. Follow the path until you reach the lane opposite the 'Dumb Post Inn'.

This curiously named pub (note the signboard) is worth visiting at this half-way point of the walk. Tucked behind the chimney breast in the far corner of the bar is a framed notice headed, 'Orders of the Friendly Society instituted at the 'Dumb Post Inn', Bremhill, on 1st January, 1770.' The bar snacks are very good here and, if you are in need of a rapid input of calories after your hike you should order the aptly named 'Jawbreaker'.

With your back to the 'Dumb Post Inn' take the road signposted to East Tytherton. At the staggered junction ahead take the left turn signposted to Chippenham. Follow this ridge top lane for about a mile ahead. The view to the south takes in the Marden valley: the course of the Calne branch of the Wilts and Berks Canal can be seen on the near side of the river — its reedy bed is easily picked out. On the far side is the course of the old Calne Branch Railway. On the hill opposite is the expanding village of Studley and, to the right and beyond, the Golden Gate of Bowood. In the valley, on rising ground just beyond the river Marden, there is much unevenness in the ground. This marks the site of the former Stanley Abbey, home of the Cistercian Order until the Dissolution of the Monasteries in 1539.

The road eventually takes you down the scarp face to the hamlet of Stanley where you recross the old Wilts and Berks Canal by Wharf Cottage. Once past the derelict Primitive Methodist Chapel you turn right along the lane signposted to West Tytherton. Follow the lane until you reach a field boundary on the right. Enter the field by the gate here and follow the hedgebank and ditch on the left. At the end of the ditch bear left to enter the adjoining field and follow the hedgebank on your right. When the hedge and ditch run out, cross the open field ahead and progress in the same direction until the ditch reappears. Again head across an open field, cross a fence and ditch and continue in the same direction towards the buildings of East Tytherton. The next ditch marks the course of the Cat Brook; now follow the hedgebank and trees on the right to reach the stile ahead. In the last field bear slightly to the left to cross the field and reach a gate on the far side. Go through the gate and follow the hedgebank on the right to reach the road through the village. Go straight ahead to reach the Moravian Chapel and the start of the walk.

8   LACOCK

via Reybridge and Lacock Bridge

Distance: 2 miles

GOING   This is an easy short walk along level field paths, much of which follows the River Avon. It includes the best way to come upon Lacock Abbey, i.e. from the north on the opposite bank of the river. The walk forms a pleasant contrast to the time you will no doubt wish to spend walking and looking around Lacock village and Abbey.

To begin the walk: take the lane leading north from the church and out of the village. You soon reach a footbridge and ford over the Bide Brook which flows just north of the village eastwards to join the River Avon. Once across the bridge you continue by the main path as it follows the brook to the right. You soon reach a house on the left where the track ends. Here you turn right and pass through a kissing gate to enter a field. Carry on by the metalled

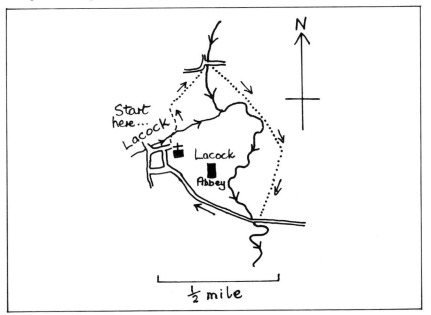

path across this field towards the houses below. There is a wide view from this path, the most prominent feature being Naish and Bowden Hills on the far side of the Avon. The lower slopes are arable fields which rise to woods in the vicinity of Bowden Park and Bewley Common.

You pass through the gate to reach the cottages and the road. Bear right to cross Rey Bridge over the Rivon Avon — note the causeway, or flood walk, for pedestrians beyond. Between the stone bridge and the causeway is a stile on the right — cross here to enter a field and follow the river downstream. The right of way crosses the field diagonally to a point just to the left of a row of crack willows bordering the river ahead. Here the river makes another bend to the right but you carry straight on towards a stile in the hedgerow beyond. Cross the stile to enter the next field and continue by following the river bank on the right — in the summer you can see teasels growing here.

Soon the river takes another twist to the right and here you must leave the river bank by walking in the same direction to reach a stile beside a gate. Head straight across the next field, to the left of the telegraph pole, towards a gap in the hedgerow ahead. The old gables of Bewley Court can be seen away to the left and Lacock Abbey begins to come into view on the right. Now head rather to the right towards a telegraph pole on the far side of this field, just below which is a squeezebelly stile by which you reach the final field before Lacock Bridge, where a gate leads you to a pavement — now bear right to reach the village.

9 BRADFORD-ON-AVON

via Greenland Mills, River Avon and Kennet and Avon Canal

Distance: 3 miles

GOING   This is an easy, short walk which leaves the historic wool town of Bradford-on-Avon and follows the river upstream past mills and factories old and new. Once past the old Greenland Mills the right of way follows a footpath behind a row of houses but soon reaches a slightly elevated field path which follows the Avon in a south-easterly direction. After descending to meet the river, the right of way rises to meet the Kennet and Avon Canal, the towpath of which takes you back towards Bradford via the locks and boat shed on Frome Road.

From the car park on the south side of the town bridge you head down Bridge Street, past the Georgian Wine Lodge and the Old Forge; notice, too, the long flight of St. Margaret's Steps on the right and an old quarry dug into the hillside. On the opposite bank of the river are the buildings of the Avon Rubber Company, partly original woollen mill buildings and partly modern buildings. Cross the railway — on your right the railway lines pass through a tunnel under St. Margaret's Hill to reach Bradford-on-Avon Station. There is a weir just below where a controlled flow of Avon water once powered the old mills on the riverbank.

Once across the railway track you bear right along a wooded footpath which gradually rises above the road. From here you look down upon some of Bradford's present-day industry: a printing works, a tennis ball factory and an engineering works, but most noticeably, upon the impressive hulk of Greenland Mills.

The footpath eventually reaches a metalled track — here you bear right to reach a stile beside a gate. Now bear left and follow the footpath at the ends of gardens on your right. Cross a stile to enter a field and follow the hedge-bank on your left, then a second stile to reach open country; once again follow the hedgebank on the left towards a third stile and continue in the same direction. The railway and river can be seen to the left. Carry on until the path takes you to a point where a boathouse faces the river, and what a peaceful spot it is. A little further upstream the Avon is joined by the River Biss, a tributary which flows through Trowbridge, another former wool town little more than a mile to the south-east.

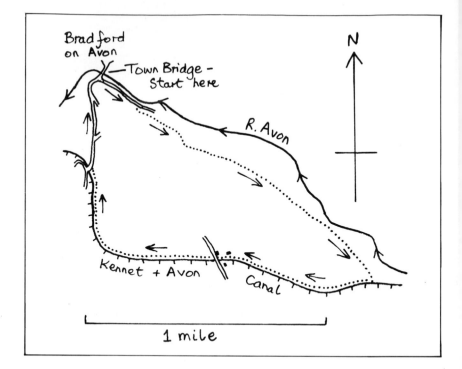

After the boathouse you must leave the river by heading directly across the field ahead towards a stile in the hedgerow. There is a brook flowing in a ditch in the hedgerow here — this is the Wid Brook which is culverted under the canal above. Head across the next field in the same direction towards another stile in the hedgerow. Once across here you can see a row of poplars ahead — this marks the course of the Kennet and Avon Canal and the next stage of the walk.

Bear right to reach the stile and the canal towpath, where you bear right. The canal environment forms a special sort of nature reserve with all the normal hedgerow plants on the 'field' side of the towpath and a variety of water loving plants on the canal banks, many of which provide homes for water fowl. An original stone bridge carries Trowbridge Road over the canal — the 'Beehive' pub is just to the right beside the road. Follow the towpath under the bridge and beyond. To the right of the next stretch is the modern housing estate of Southway Park but the canal and towpath are so well shielded by trees and shrubs, as well as being in a shallow cutting that you really are unaware of the fact that you are passing along the edge of a built-up area.

After passing under a new road bridge there is the entrance to a former quarry on the left which unfortunately, at the time of writing, has been all but filled with rubbish. Clay was formerly extracted from here for use in 'puddling' the canal to make the bed and banks watertight. This clay is known as the Bradford Clay, a local variation of the Forest Marble formation and is found interbedded with coarse, fossiliferous beds of limestone.

You reach the locks and boat shed at Frome Road, with 'The Barge' pub to the left and 'The Canal Tavern' to the right across the road. Now bear right and follow Frome Road back towards the town bridge.

10 BRADFORD-ON-AVON

via Belcombe, Turleigh, Avoncliff, Kennet and Avon Canal and Barton Farm Country Park

Distance: 3 miles

GOING   This is an easy short walk along the valley of the Avon from Bradford as far as Avoncliff where the Kennet and Avon Canal crosses the river and railway by means of an aqueduct. There is a gradual ascent from Belcombe to Turleigh, then a steeper climb down to the aqueduct. The lane leaving Avoncliff on the opposite bank is steep too, but this may be avoided by following the canal towpath. There are tea gardens and a pub 'The Cross Guns' at Avoncliff.

The car park beyond Bradford-on-Avon railway station is a good starting point for this walk. At the very end of the car park you will find a footpath which takes you directly to the riverbank. Bear left under the railway bridge and then follow the river downstream towards the old pack horse bridge. Barton Farm is the large building ahead to the left and behind that you can see the great stone-tiled roof of the tithe barn.

Cross the bridge over the river and cross the field by the footpath which bears to the left (not the one which leads directly to the kissing gate and railway crossing). Follow this path beside the fence on the right. As you approach the top of the field bear right towards a wooden kissing gate and cross the railway tracks. Now the path bears left beside the railway, then right to reach the road.

Turn left here and follow the pavement on the far side. You soon pass the entrance gates to Balcombe Court. It is difficult to see very much of this beautiful house over the high wall which borders the lane but you may catch a glimpse of the magnificent south front set off by four Ionic pilasters. John Wood the Elder added this wing to an older house in 1734 for Francis Yerbury, a local clothier. The main complex of buildings includes a medieval barn and near the main façade is a domed rotunda and grotto. The grounds extend to the west behind the stone wall.

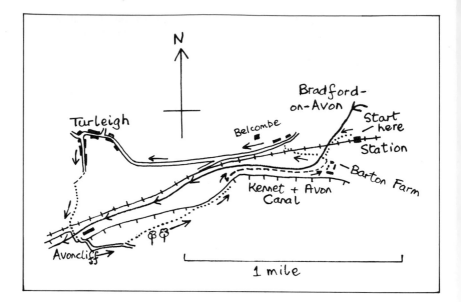

The road reaches a fork, the left turning of which presents the most direct (and easiest) route to Avoncliff, but our way follows the lane rising straight ahead towards Turleigh. You are soon rewarded with a view across and down the valley towards Avoncliff and straight on towards Turleigh, whose buildings form a V on either side of a cleft in the valley here. Turleigh could fairly be described as picturesque: all is now neatly residential but the names of some of the dwellings reveal the varied uses to which many of them were formerly put, e.g. Malt House, Old Post Office, Old Tannery.

Continue to follow the road through the village until you reach a junction. The village main street bears to the right and is signposted to Winsley, Limpley Stoke and Bath. Here your turn left. As you begin to descend you bear right along the track signposted to Elbow Cottage. This track soon reaches a gate beside which is an old and bent iron kissing gate. Once through here bear left and descend the field towards Avoncliff. As you descend you will see up the valley and back towards Bradford. On the far side of the valley is Becky Addy Wood through which we shall return from Avoncliff. Soon you can hear the roar of the Avon passing over the weir. You should bear rather to the right above the fence at the bottom of the field — the exit is by another kissing gate in the bottom right-hand corner. From here you follow the footpath downhill to reach the lane and the canal.

Cross the aqueduct over the railway lines and the Avon to reach the opposite bank. The 'Cross Guns' pub is on your left, the tea gardens are on your right and the canal towpath straight ahead. The towpath is the direct and easy route from here but our route bears left here towards the pub, then left again and under the aqueduct, then left once again to reach the lane out of Avoncliff. Follow this lane uphill until you reach a signpost indicating a public footpath through a wood to the left. If you can bear to climb a further

124

25 yards or so uphill by the lane you can see the entrance to a former stone mine. This is reached via the next opening on the right by a sunken track on the left.

Follow the wide, well-worn footpath down through the woods. Soon there is a fork — take the right fork to continue by the edge of the woods, not left into a field. Simply follow the footpath by the edge of the wood with its view over the valley on the left until you reach a stile to enter a field. Head diagonally across this field to reach a stile in the bottom left-hand corner. This point is just beside the canal and you may notice that the stone 'step' here has the letters 'KA' inscribed in it. Now follow the left-hand edge of the next field towards a stile, then the footpath beside the canal towards a swing bridge. Cross the canal here and descend towards the Avon by the metalled track and follow this track back towards Barton Farm and the pack horse bridge. From here you retrace your footsteps under the railway bridge and back to the station car park

11   DUNDAS AQUEDUCT

via River Avon, Warleigh Woods and Conkwell

Distance: 3 miles

GOING   This is a short and fairly easy walk which includes the longest section of riverside path between Bradford-on-Avon and Bath. There is a steady climb up through Warleigh Woods by a quiet lane and then a much sharper descent through the hamlet of Conkwell and by track and field path to return to Dundas Aqueduct. There are no churches or other points of great historic or architectural interest — it is rather a most pleasant country ramble which affords some magnificent views of the Avon valley.

The starting point for this ramble is the long layby on the east side of the A36 south of Claverton and a little to the north of 'The Viaduct' public house at the turning for Monkton Combe. At the south end of the layby you take the track which is signposted 'Public Footpath' to reach a basin on the Kennet and Avon Canal. The old Somerset Coal Canal joined the K and A at this point. Follow the towpath on the left, past the old crane, to reach the footbridge across the canal. On the far side follow the towpath to cross the aqueduct.

At a point about twenty yards before the hut on the side of the canal look out for a rough path leading away to the left and down the canal embankment to cross a stile and reach the field below, just to the right of the boathouse. Now follow the riverside path downstream, across one wooden stile to enter the next field, then through a gate and across a stream to a third field, then to a crossing point into one more field. As you approach the end of this field bear right to reach a track under a horse chestnut tree until you reach a cluster of farm buildings. From here you can see across the valley to Claverton, the village spread along the hillside and the old manor house, now the American Museum, standing close to the wooded hilltop. Down the valley Bathford Hill on the east faces Bathampton Down on the west, both well wooded and, beyond them, Little Solsbury Hill and Charmy Down.

As you approach the farm buildings you come to a gate by which you enter the farmyard. Now bear left to leave the farm and reach the lane. Here you turn sharp right by the stone which is inscribed 'Sheephouse Farm'. Now you begin to ascend the hill through Warleigh Wood — this lane is a tunnel of green in the summer with the spreading branches arching over from either side.

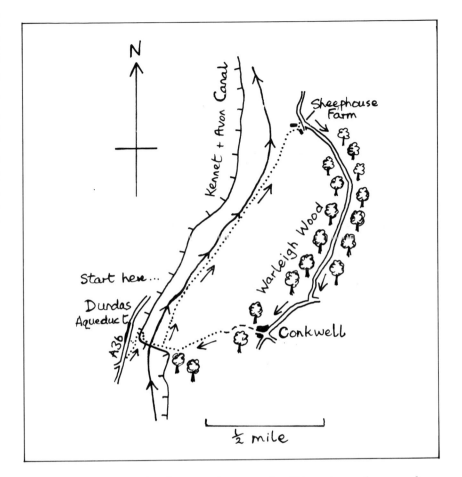

Eventually the lane levels out and you reach a T junction — here you bear right to reach Conkwell, then right again to descend the village 'main street'. At Spring Cottage you head down the track to the right. This is a sunken way and descends steeply. Follow the wood on the left until you reach a stile on the left beside a trough. Cross the stile and head diagonally across the sloping field towards the bottom left-hand corner. Here you will find access to a wide track which descends the hill to meet the canal towpath just below — there is a stile to cross before this is reached. Carry on to recross the aqueduct and retrace your steps back to the main road.

12 KELSTON

via Kelston Mills, River Avon, North Stoke, slopes of Lansdown, Kelston Round Hill and Dean Hill.

Distance: 5½ miles

GOING   Notwithstanding their vulnerable position between Bath and Bristol, Kelston and North Stoke are villages which retain a good deal of individuality and character. Kelston perhaps suffers from sitting astride the main road whilst North Stoke is hidden away at the end of a lane which climbs from that road halfway up Lansdown. The way across the slopes of Lansdown and Kelston Round Hill is easy to follow, exhilarating and most enjoyable. The crossing points are often marked by iron gates of unusually elaborate design and you feel that these ways were well trodden in the eighteenth and nineteenth centuries by visitors to the spa town of Bath. This route passes near, but does not actually reach the renowned Prospect Stile — this must be one of the few such to be named and marked on an O.S. map. From our route this is reach only by crossing a large cornfield and this I have avoided. The prospect, especially from the ridge connecting Lansdown and Kelston Round Hill, is surely one outstanding enough! There is a pub in Kelston but none in North Stoke.

As you approach Kelston from Bath, take the first left in the village towards the church or, from Bristol, the first right past the pub. There is plenty of room to park in this street which leads to Manor Farm and the village church. St. Nicholas is usually kept locked. The square, squat tower is medieval but most of the rest is a Victorian rebuilding. Some interesting Roman remains in the shape of a small coffin can be seen in the porch. In the grounds of Manor Farm, adjacent to the church, is a large stone barn.

Retracing your footsteps from the church you bear left at the bottom of the slope. Once past 'The Old School House' on the right you go through a gate to enter a field. Walk past a barn on the right in the direction of a gate in the far right corner. As you cross the field you can see Saltford across the valley to the west and Keynsham beyond. Leave this field by a kissing gate and continue by the track opposite. Look out for a gate about 150 yards down on the right. Head straight across and down this large and irregularly shaped field to reach a stile near the far right corner. Now follow a track between hedgebanks to reach a lane which leads you down to Kelston Mills on the River Avon.

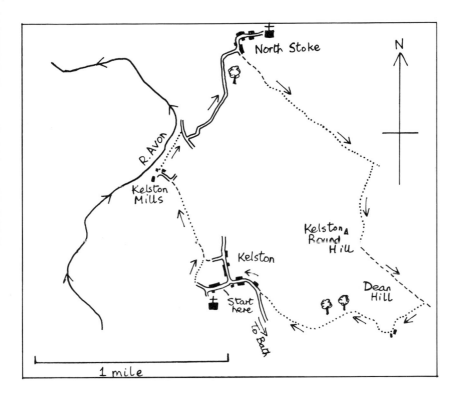

Facing the twin annealing towers of the former brass mill, make for a gate between cottages on the right. Now follow the river downstream towards a stile about 20 yards from the far left corner. Cross here and head through the next field to reach the road in the top right corner. Turn right at the road and follow the pavement the short distance to reach the lane on the left to North Stoke. The lane climbs steadily but not too painfully the ¾ mile to the village. You will surely want to reach the church at the top of the village before continuing with the next stage of the walk.

If so, bear left at the T-junction and follow the lane up to the diminutive Church of St. Martin. The view west and south is terrific and the churchyard is an ideal place to spread out your map and pick out the landmarks. The church has another of those short squat towers, so untypical of North Somerset but not unlike those at Kelston and Saltford. The church contains several memorial tablets, not particularly old or fine but which make interesting, if sometimes poignant reading.

Facing the T-junction near the bottom of the village bear right. The metalled lane reverts to a stony track after the last house. As you crest the hill the track and the view south opens out — if it is a sunny day the glistening surface of the Avon between Saltford and Kelston Mill will catch your eye. Continue by this fenced path for almost a mile. You eventually reach a point where there is a turning to the right which seems to lead towards a point to the right of the conical hill crowned with trees ahead, i.e. Kelston Round Hill. Do not take this track but carry straight on until you reach an iron gate. Go through this iron gate, then a second and turn right to follow the hedge-bank on your right. Kelston Round Hill is straight ahead and the path follows a ridge connecting it with Lansdown. The view is a panorama: south-east is Weston and the valley leading towards the centre of Bath while west is the Avon valley and its towns and villages.

This right of way continues to follow the hedgebank on the right through two field boundaries and then bends to the left towards Dean Hill. Straight ahead is an uninterrupted view towards Bath. Look out for a gate on the right a little less than half a mile from the bend. Head across the field towards a gate in the hedge opposite. Cross here and head diagonally across the bottom of the next field towards a gate — now follow the hedgebank on the right towards the house ahead. Just before the house turn right across a stile. Walk across this field towards a gate in the far left corner just below the hanging wood. Continue straight on by the worn footpath to reach a gate on the far side. Where the track forks take the left fork down towards the gate. Simply follow the right of way along a fairly even contour about 25 yards below the hanging woods.

You will see the plain Georgian house of Kelston Park just below on a bluff overlooking the Avon. The twin towers of Kelston village are straight ahead. The less significant one on the left belongs to the church; the other to the Victorian Tower House on the main road. Go through the gate on the far side of the field, then head across and down the last field, not directly towards the road but towards a stony track which leads to the road. Now follow the pavement to Tower House where you turn left to reach the church.

13 HANHAM MILLS

via River Avon, Hencliff Wood and Hanham Court

Distance: 3 miles
Extension or alternative walk to river below Willsbridge
Distance: 2½ miles
GOING   Hanham Gorge and Woods are not as dramatic as Avon Gorge
and Leigh Woods on the west side of Bristol but they are nevertheless most
attractive and, because there is no road through the valley here, a great deal
quieter. The Avon, although tidal, does not exhibit the great rise and fall
which it does west of the city and its character is still of a country river rather
than a shipping lane or estuary. The towpath from Hanham Mills to a point
below Conham, before the river banks show any signs of industry, is an
easy, level walk. The return is through the woods, by the edge of suburbia
and through fields to Hanham Court. From here you can follow the lane
back down to Hanham Mills and the pubs 'The Chequers Inn' and 'The
Old Lock and Weir'. Alternatively, you can continue by a simple route
through fields to a point on the Avon opposite Keynsham Hams and thence
by riverside meadows below hanging woods to return to Hanham Mills.

From the large car park at Hanham Mills you head downstream by the
towpath on the right bank. You pass two pubs, one rather grander than the
other, some mill cottages and Hanham Lock where the river meets the tidal
Avon. Now follow the towpath along the wooded valley for about 1½ miles.
The left bank begins to flatten out from the rather high and steep aspect it
has presented since Hanham Mills, and ahead you can see quarries in the
side of the hill which rises to Conham — the river swings to the left to avoid
this hill. The next stage of the route is marked by a public footpath sign
indicating Hanham Common along a track to the right.

Follow this footpath uphill — avoiding branches down again to the river.
Where a branch heads to the left by a marker stone inscribed 'H 1876' you
head straight on. (You may be interested to follow the left track for a short
distance to reach a small disused quarry in the Pennant Sandstone.) The
path ahead gradually rises until you meet a house on the left before the path
ends at a road. Turn right here along a track with new houses on your left
and the woods on your right. You reach a stile with a notice 'Mowing Grass
— Keep to the Footpath'. Cross this stile to enter the field and bear left
below the house until you reach the far left corner.

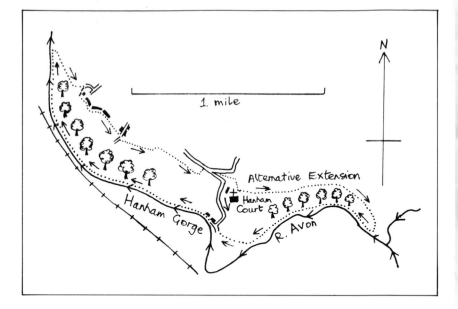

Cross here and follow the path between the back gardens of the houses on the left and the hedgerow on the right. Carry on until you reach the lane where there are some older houses. Here you bear right, then immediately left — now look out for a public footpath sign on your left. Cross the stile and head straight across this field to pass a couple of pig-sties, a rare sight nowadays, and leave by a stile under a telegraph pole. Now you descend through some woods, cross a brook and turn left. A signpost here indicates rights of way in every direction, including skyward! Turn right to ascend the slope to reach a field. Now follow the hedgebank on the left. As you approach the stone wall in the far corner of the field you must bear left to reach the road. Now turn right to reach the avenue of trees on the triangle between the main road and the lane down to Hanham Mills.

Hanham Court is reached by walking down the avenue of limes to reach a kissing gate beneath an arch in the stone wall. Once through here you can see the lodge house to the right and Hanham Court and Church a little beyond. Reach the road by the gate ahead and bear right towards the church.

13.1 Extension or alternative walk to River Avon below Willsbridge.

Distance: 2½ miles

Facing Hanham church, retrace your steps up the drive for a few yards until you spot the iron gate on the right with a public footpath sign indicating Willsbridge. Go through the gate and follow the hedged path up the slope until you reach the kissing gate at the top. Now enter a field and carry straight on. There is a wide view from here, especially south over the Avon valley towards Keynsham. Head straight towards the wood and simply follow the fieldpath by keeping the boundary of the wood immediately on your right.

Eventually the edge of the wood descends the slope towards the river and you follow it down to a corner where you pass through a gate and follow a green track directly to the Avon. The Fry's Chocolate factory is on the far side across the flat meadows known as Keynsham Hams. There is a signpost indicating Conham along the towpath to the right. Follow the river until you reach the end of the wood — now follow the right-hand boundary of the field if you wish to avoid walking the long way round the pronounced bend in the river here. The car park at Hanham Mills is straight ahead.

14 LEIGH WOODS

via Paradise Bottom, Avon Gorge and Nightingale Valley

Distance: 4 miles

GOING   A walk through woods by way of a valley named after our most famous songbird, a gorge containing the River Avon and a bottom, or valley, named after heaven itself surely cannot fail to delight! This route, so near the city of Bristol, hardly passes a building and provides a fascinating route for the nature lover as well as for those wanting to explore the gorge. Although there is a difference in altitude of some 300 feet from the starting point to the Avon and back up again the descent and ascent are not over-strenuous. All the previous walks have, for the sake of consistency in a book entitled *Down the Bristol Avon*, followed the river downstream. This one, however, follows the river in the opposite direction for the reason that the route is easier to follow that way.

The nearest pub is 'The George Inn' on the main road at Abbots Leigh. The village is strung out along a minor road along a ridge. The church of Holy Trinity and the view from there along the Avon towards the docks and the Bristol Channel is worth seeing.

Access by car to Leigh Woods is gained from the A369 from Ashton Gate or Clifton Bridge. Continue along the main road, cross over the traffic lights and look out for a signpost indicating 'Forestry Commission — Stoke Leigh Woods — Car Park and Forest Walks'. Bear right here and follow the straight, roughly surfaced avenue for 800 yards to reach the car park. Here, there is a board with a map showing two recommended walks through the woods. Our way follows the red route downhill but leaves it to reach the towpath in the Avon Gorge. So, from the car park walk straight on, heading gradually downhill. After a little over half a mile the track forks. The way to the left is marked by a red arrow — the official route. Our way bears right to head downhill. You suddenly emerge from the trees to a view north along the Avon. The forest track all but meets the towpath but you must negotiate a stone wall which forms the boundary of the forest in order to reach it. The old Portishead branch railway passes through a tunnel at this point. If you care to digress a little then bear left, downstream, and there you will find a four-arched viaduct which carries the old line across the mouth of Paradise Bottom.

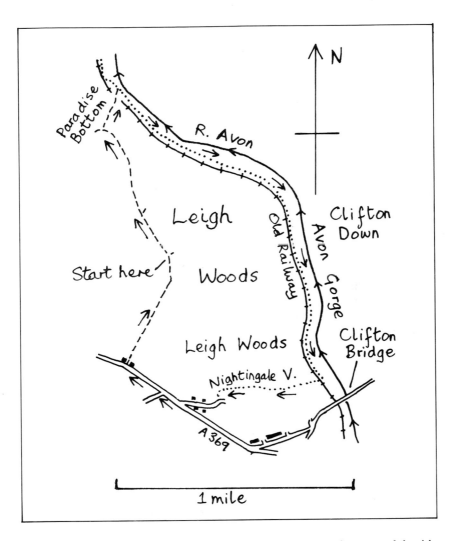

N

Paradise Bottom

R. Avon

Leigh

Start here

Woods

Leigh Woods

Nightingale V.

Old Railway

Avon Gorge

Clifton Down

Clifton Bridge

A 369

1 mile

To continue the walk bear right, upstream, and follow the towpath beside the river for almost two miles to a point just before Clifton suspension Bridge. This way gives the most spectacular views of the Gorge: the rock face opposite, although broken by a number of clefts, for the most part rises sheer from the river valley to the plateau like Clifton Downs. Whilst the left bank is almost all clothed with woods, except where quarries have exposed the strata, the right bank is mainly naked rock. Less than half a mile before Clifton Bridge, Valley Bridge Road ascends a cleft towards the Down — the Observatory can be seen crowning the cliffs a little further upstream. The limestone strata can be seen to be dipping at an angle of about 30°. Between the main bulk of dipping strata and Valley Bridge Road there is a band of darker coloured and crumpled strata — this marks a major fault.

Clifton Suspension Bridge, that amazing creation of Brunel's, seems to loom ever higher as you approach from the north. You should look out for an arch under the railway on your right about 200 yards before a point directly beneath the bridge. Leave the towpath here to enter the wood and continue by following the track straight ahead along the bottom of Nightingale Valley. This is a deep and steep-sided valley, particularly on the south where the sylvan scenery is spectacular — less a hanging wood than a suspended wood!

At the top of the path bear left to reach the stile, then right to reach the main road. Here you turn right and follow the road across the traffic lights opposite Beggar Bush Lane. The avenue to the car park is just past the former entrance gateway to Leigh Court, with its four massive Ionic columns, on the right.